ANTHOLOGY OF SERBIAN POETRY:
THE GOLDEN AGE

ANTHOLOGY OF SERBIAN POETRY:
THE GOLDEN AGE

by

MIHAILO DORDEVIC

Philosophical Library
New York

Library of Congress Cataloging in Publication Data

Main entry under title:

Anthology of Serbian poetry.

English and Serbo-Croatian in parallel columns.
1. Serbian poetry—19th century. 2. Serbian poetry—
20th century. 3. Serbian poetry—Translations into
English. 4. English poetry—Translation from Serbo-
Croatian. I. Dordevic, Mihailo.
PG1595.E3A5   1984   891.8'214'08   84-7672
ISBN 0-8022-2467-9

Published, 1984, by Philosophical Library, Inc.,
200 West 57 Street, New York, N.Y. 10019.
Copyright 1984 by Mihailo Dordevic.
All rights reserved.
Manufactured in the United States of America.

To the memory of my late father
Dr. Vladimir Dordević
and to my mother
Jelena, nee Rašić,
with love and respect

Contents / vii

Jovan Dučić (1871-1943)

Aleksa Šantić (1868-1924)

x / antologija srpske poezije

There are many reasons for the publication of an *Anthology of Serbian Poetry*, especially that of the *Golden Age* (1880-1914). That the poems be published simultaneously in both the original language and in their English translation is a necessity for intercultural understanding. Some of the Serbian poems from this period have been published in translation in the United States, but not recently. Furthermore, these have been disseminated throughout many different literary periodicals and reviews, and are not readily accessible to most readers. I have voluntarily abstained from reading these translations for fear of being influenced by them. All translations in this *Anthology* are original and have not been previously published.

A bilingual anthology of Serbian poetry reaches multiple fields of interest. There are numerous courses in Serbo-Croatian language and literature offered at Departments of Slavic and East European Studies at many American universities. This anthology will be helpful to students in this particular field. In addition, there is a vast number of Americans of Yugoslav ethnic background who are interested in the poetry and culture of their country of origin. Their lack of knowledge of Serbo-Croatian prevents them from reading these poems in their original form. Furthermore, the poems in their original language will now be available to older Serbo-Croatian emigrés who know the language and wish to retain ties with their cultural heritage. Anthologies of Serbian poetry, especially of that period, have not been published recently either in America or Yugoslavia. They are, therefore, scarce and difficult to obtain in both countries.

Serbian poetry at the turn of the century presents a wealth of aesthetic experience. It broadens the scope of international poetry. Even readers who otherwise have no ethnic or academic interest in the literature of the Balkans will have an opportunity to enjoy a rich new field of poetry. Along with the aesthetic and creative challenge such a work presented, these cultural and practical considerations were basic to my desire to offer this *Anthology of Serbian Poetry* to the English speaking world.

The selection of poems was based on the presentation of works of important and innovative poets of this period. The choice of poems was dependent upon the introduction of new themes into the modernization of Serbian nineteenth-century poetry, as well as upon the original contribution to the development of a modern versification. For this reason, a number of aesthetically valid poems were excluded from this *Anthology* if, and when, they did not represent the growth in modernism.

The poets and their works are not presented in this *Anthology* either in alphabetical or chronological order. Rather, an effort has been made to present the poets according to the thematic content of their poems, the development of schools, and the introduction of new mood patterns into the Serbian poetry at the turn of the century.

The *Anthology* begins with the poems of Vojislav Ilić who represented the new movement which succeeded the Romanticism in the Serbian poetry of the 1860s and 1870s.

Djura Jakšić, although essentially a poet of the Romantic period, was chosen because of his theme of personal grief and pessimism which led to the poetry of Velimir Rajić. These poems are followed by the work of Milan Rakić and Jovan Dučić who created and almost imposed the eleven-and twelve-syllable verse on the Serbian poetry of the *Golden Age*. The new versification which replaced Vojislav Ilić's sixteen syllable verse became the hallmark of modern Serbian poetry. For this reason, and because Rakić and Dučić represent the peak of poetry in the early twentieth century, they are represented by the largest number of poems in the *Anthology*. The poems of Aleksa Šantić close the first period of the *Golden Age* of Serbian poetry.

The further development of this period is represented by the poems which do not belong to any particular school or versification. Vojislav Ilić-Mladji was chosen for his partial return to Serbian Romanticism, while the other poets, Veljko Petrović, Miloš Perović, Stevan Luković, Svetislav Stefanović, Milan Ćurčin, and Milutin Bojić were selected as examples of the further modernization of Serbian poetry. The abrupt conclusion of the *Golden Age* was brought about by World War I and the fusion after the war of Serbia, Croatia, and Slovenia into the new kingdom of the Southern Slavs, known today as Yugoslavia.

Only five poems by Vojislav Ilić were included. The poetry of Ilić was a break that occurred between the Romantic poetry of the nineteenth century and the beginnings of the new, modern Serbian poetry of the turn of the century. *On the River Vardar* was chosen as an example of the nationalistic and patriotic poetry which was so vital to the Romantic poetry of the nineteenth century. Thematically, and by tonality, it belongs to the Romantic style. Ilić's *Untitled Poem* ("With eyes spent and unseeing...") was chosen because it introduced into modern Serbian poetry the motif of modern pessimism and the alienation of the poet from the society of his time. This motif became more frequent in the development of Serbian poetry in the following decades. The two other poems by Ilić were selected because they represent his talent in painting images of nature and lead to *Autumnal Strolls* by Bojić. A simple comparison of these poems shows the range in versification of Ilić to Bojić.

The choice of only five poems by Ilić does not attempt to diminish the pivotal and essential role he played in setting the stage for the development of the modern Serbian poetry in the early twentieth century. Though numerous, Ilić's poems which deal with ancient civilizations are represented by a single poem: *Gypsy*. Poems with themes from history are represented in later Serbian poetry. However, they show no trace of Ilić's influence nor do they represent his escapism into the aesthetic dream of bygone days.

The technical problems encountered by a translator when he must alter original poems by transposing them into the music of another language offer two alternatives. The decision was made to transpose poetic images and attempt to keep primarily the rhythm and the poetic tonality of the original for this *Anthology*. Since the rendering of the total aesthetic experience represented by the poems in the original is the unaccessible dream of every translator, the transposition over the literal translation, which appears to be the least damaging to the poetry, was the course chosen. The alternative would have been to translate *verbatim* while trying to keep the exact number of syllables, and, ideally, the rhyme.

In this respect difficulties seemed to be less ominous with poems written in a depictive, direct discourse method. As French Symbolism, at its peak in the 1880s, introduced the evocative, fluid, indirect discourse method, it made the work of translators more difficult. Aside from the euphonic qualities of words and the evocative secondary connotations which all words have, cultural and literary barriers play an important role in Symbolistic poetry. Many of the Serbian poems written under the influence of the Symbolist school and of its Instrumentalist subdivision do not represent thought-governed emotional experiences, but deal with spontaneous, conflicting moods.

Svetislav Stefanović's *Musical Visions* contains as little thought structure as Monet's *Waterlilies* paintings of which they immediately remind this reader. In visual arts and music, the resistance of the artistic medium is far less dominant than it is in the medium of language. The aim of language as an accepted convention among human beings to communicate thoughts and emotions loses this element of direct communication with the arrival of the symbolist evocative and personal interpretation of individual moods. The further development of this conflict between musicality and communication of thought structure leads eventually to the Futurist poems by Marinetti and to the non-objective or abstract forms in the visual arts of the twentieth century. The direct attack on the object, *per se,* that began with the Impressionists, led to an attack against syntax and grammar as means of object-communication through thought structures in the field of poetry. This accounts for the essential difficulty in transposing Stefanović's *Musical Visions* from one language into another. If the transposition of Aleksa Šantić's *Evening at Školje* falls far short of the beauty of the original text, it was, nevertheless, included in this *Anthology* because of the importance of this poem as a milestone in the achievement of modern Serbian versification. It demonstrates the breadth between Kaćanski's and Aberdar's poetry, and that of the modern Serbian poetry at the turn of the century. A number of other symbolistic poems have been included for the same reason, regardless of the euphonic and evocative difficulties such transpositions presented.

There was a strong desire not to overextend this *Anthology* but to include in it only the most significant achievements of Serbian poetry at the turn of the century. This

Anthology is far from representative of all the best of Serbian poetry of this period. The choice of these poetic works was, therefore, personal and arbitrary.

Vojislav ILIĆ   1860 / 1894

Na Vardaru

Suro, večito stenje gordo se u nebo diže;
Nad urvinama tavnim orli se s oblakom bore.
A dole sa strašnim šumom Vardar se peni, i stiže
I pada kroz uske klance u sinje Jegejsko More.
O vali, o reko srpska! Stoleća tako se gube,
I kao talasi tonu u more večnosti tavne.
Al' tvoje biserne kaplje kamena podnožja ljube
Gde spomenici stoje narodne prošlosti slavne.
Ali će, k'o rajski feniks, sinuti sloboda mila;
I ja ću stajati vedar gde sada pogružen stojim,
I naš će or'o beli široko razviti krila
    Nad urvinama tvojim.

Vojislav Ilić

On the River Vardar

Dark, eternal boulders soar proudly to the skies;
High above somber gulfs eagles fight the clouds.
Beneath them with a terrifying rumble Vardar foams and
    runs
And falls through narrow ravines into the blue Aegean Sea.
Oh waves, oh Serbian river! Centuries vanish so,
And sink like waves into the sea of somber eternity.
But your drops like pearls forever kiss the foothills
On which stand memorials of the glorious national past.
Some day, like the heavenly phoenix, freedom will dawn
And I shall stand serene where I now stand humbled
And our white eagle will spread his wings wide
To span your somber gulfs.

Vojislav Ilić

*　　*　　*

Sa pogledom ugašenim,
S prekrštenim rukama,
Na mrtvačkom odru svom
Ležao sam medj' vama.

Vi ste moje bledo lice
Rosnim vencem obvili,
I o mojim bolovima
Sa uzdahom zborili.

Ja sam sluš'o reči vaše
S njinim slatkim otrovom,
I gorko sam nasmej'o se
Pod mrtvačkim pokrovom.

Vojislav Ilić

*   *   *

With eyes spent and unseeing,
With arms folded on my chest,
In my coffin I was lying,
Among you to take my rest.

You adorned my ashen head
With pale flowers for the dead;
You spoke of my torments
With false tears and loud laments.

I listened to what you said,
To your words that sounded sad,
Then bitterly laughed aloud
Under cover of my shroud.

Vojislav Ilić

U poznu jesen

Čuj kako jauče vetar kroz puste poljane naše,
   I guste slojeve magle u vlažni valja dô...
Sa krikom uzleće gavran i kruži nad mojom glavom;
   Mutno je nebo svo.

Frkće okis'o konjic i žurno u selo grabi,
   I već pred sobom vidi ubog i stari dom.
Na pragu starica stoji i mokru živinu vabi,
   I s repom kosmatim svojim ogroman zeljov s njom; —

A vetar sumorno zviždi kroz crna i pusta polja,
   I guste slojeve magle u vlažni valja dô...
Sa krikom uzleće gavran i kruži nad mojom glavom;
   Mutno je nebo svo.

Vojislav Ilić

Late Fall

Listen to the wind howl across our desolate fields,
    And roll deep layers of fog into our damp valley...
With a shriek a raven takes off and circles above my head;
    Leaden is the sky.

A rain-soaked horse snorts and hurries back to the village,
    Looking forward to his old and humble home.
On the threshold an old woman stands and calls the wet
    fowl,
    By her side a big grey mutt with a shaggy tail; —

The wind hisses somberly across the desolate black fields;
    And rolls deep layers of fog into the damp valley...
With a shriek a raven takes off and circles above my head;
    Leaden is the sky.

Vojislav Ilić

Sivo, sumorno nebo. Sa starih ograda davno
Uveli ladolež već je sumorno spustio vreže;
A dole, skrhane vetrom, po zemlji grančice leže;

Sve mračna obori jesen, i sve je pusto i tavno;
Bez života sve je.
Izgleda kao da samrt prirodu steže,
I ona tiho mre...

A po kaljavom drumu, pogružen u smernoj tugi,
Ubogi sprovod se kreće. Mršavo maleno kljuse
Lagano taljige vuče, a vrat je pružilo dugi...
I kiša dosadno sipi, i sprovod prolazi tako,
Pobožno i polako.

Vojislav Ilić

The sky is grey and gloomy. For days now
The wilted honeysuckle trails down the old fences;
And below, broken by the winds, tiny twigs lie on the
    ground;

The somber fall smothered everything; all is barren, dark;
    Without any life.
It seems tired nature fell into the grip of agony,
    Where it slowly dies.

While on the muddy road, mournful in unassuming grief,
A humble funeral passes. Bony and withered, a nag
Pulls the peasant cart slowly, straining its long neck...
The tiresome rain drizzles, while the funeral passes
    Pious and slow.

Vojislav Ilić

Ciganče

Bezbrižno i milo dete! podigni vitice svoje!
Kako si čupava strašno! Ah, tvoje usnice rujne,
I strasno, vatreno oko, i grudi sveže i bujne
    Vesele oko moje.

Dodaj mi zlatan pehar! Iz tvojih očiju, lane,
Ja čitam strasnu povest, koje se mnogi još seća:
Kad Bahus podiže vojsku na plodne indijske strane,
    Na zemlje mirisnog cveća.

U vihorima strasti, sa divljom, pomamnom vikom,
Skakaše bezumna vojska od ljudi, žena i zveri,
Drevne indijske gore oglašavahu krikom
    Istoka bujne kćeri...

Ciganče, tako mi Baha! i ja sam medj' njima bio!
No ti mi objasni sada: šta činim ovo, i gdi sam?
Ja vidim da sam pijan, i ako — zašto bih krio —
    Dirnuo pehar nisam.

Vojislav Ilić

Gypsy

Carefree sweet child! Straighten your curls!
How terribly disheveled you are! Oh, your red lips!
And passionate, fiery eyes, your young lush breasts,
    Rejoice my eyes.

Hand me the golden goblet! In your eyes, sweet child,
I read the passionate story which many men recall;
How Bacchus and his host invaded the fertile Hindu land,
    This country of fragrant blossoms.

Whirling with passion, with wild and frantic screams,
The senseless host leaped, men, women and beasts.
The ancient Hindu forests announced with howls
    The coming of the lush daughters of the East.

My little gypsy, by Bacchus I swear! I was among them, too!
But tell me now: what am I doing and where am I?
I see I am drunk, though—why not admit it?—
    I did not touch the goblet.

Vojislav Ilić

Djura JAKŠIĆ   1832 / 1878

Gde ja...

Gde ja šećer sijem,
Tu otrov izrasti;
Gde ja pevat' mnijem,
Tu ću u plač pasti.

Gde na druga brojim,
Tu krvnika imam,
Gde ja lovor svojim,
Trnov venac primam.

—Skori sveća kraju,
Danak crnoj noći,
Al' kraj mome vaju
Nikad neće doći.

Djura Jakšić

Where I...

Where I spread sugar
There I harvest poison;
Where I intend to sing
There I burst into tears.

Where I count on a friend
There I find a foe;
Where I expect a wreath
There I get a crown of thorns.

—The candle is near its end
The day close to the dark night;
But the end of my sorrows
Will never come for me.

Djura Jakšić

Velimir RAJIĆ   1879 / 1915

Rasklapa zora...

Rasklapa zora trepavice sane,
I budi danak sa svojega krila:
"Ustani, dragi, noć je veće bila!"
I danak sluša, i pokorno svane,

I krvav istok svom silinom plane.
U sobi tama. Maloga kandila
Poslednji zraci, meki kao svila,
Umiru; nema ko ulja da kane...

Kandilo moje, mi smo sreće jedne:
I moje grudi za životom žedne,
K'o ti za uljem; moj duh svake noći,

I svakog dana, i svakoga časka,
Puckara, pišti—ali toga glaska
Nit' čuju, niti mu mogu pomoći...

Velimir Rajić

Dawn Unfolds...

Dawn unfolds her heavy lashes,
And wakes the day asleep on her lap:
"Rise, my lover, night is here no more!"
The day obeys and rises humbly,

And Orient, bleeding, breaks into flames.
The room is dark. From the small votive lamp
The last rays, tender as soft silk,
Die slowly; there is no one to add oil...

My votive lamp, we are both ill-fated:
My own breast longs for life
As you crave oil; my soul each night,

And each day, and at every moment,
Flickers and sputters—but this frail voice
No one hears and no one can help...

Velimir Rajić

Zavet

Kada umrem—smrt će skoro doći,
Još tren koji, pa će zakucati
I na moga života tamnicu:
Te rastočit' železne okove
Što mi dušu od postanka stežu,
I spasti je ropstva večitoga—
Nemojte mi ruke prekrstiti,
Jer mi živom behu zavezane.

Nemojte me u crkvu nositi—
Jer kad god sam u Boga molio
Da me spase nevolje očajne,
On se svagda molbi oglušio.
Već me pravo groblju ponesite,
Kopajte mi raku preduboku,
Da me mrtva ne ogrije sunce;
Jer moj život studena je zima;
Nek' mi bude od zemljice toplo.

Čelo glave krst mi ne stavljajte,
Jer sam bio raspet za života;
Već naval'te gomilu kamenja,
Nek' se diže do neba visoko!
Pa kad dodje čas Strašnoga Suda,
I kad mrtvi počnu ustajati,
Neka tada sve groblje oživi—
Kamen nek' mi pritisne grobnicu,
Samo da se ja dići ne mogu.

Dying Wish

When I die—and death will come soon,
And in a moment or two knock on the door
Of the cell in which my life is locked,
To break loose the shackles and chains
That have bound my soul since birth,
And lift it from eternal slavery—
Let not my arms be folded then
For they were shackled all my life.

Carry me not to church—
For when I prayed to God
To spare me hopeless anguish
He stayed deaf to all my prayers.
But carry me straight to the graveyard.
Dig me a grave as deep as you can.
Let not the sun warm me in death
For my life is ice-cold winter,
Let me feel the warmth of the earth.

Put no cross at the head of my grave,
For I was crucified in life;
Pile a heap of heavy stones,
And let them rise to high heavens!
And when Judgment Day arrives,
And the dead begin to rise,
The whole graveyard will come to life,
Then let the stones weigh down my grave,
So that I alone cannot arise.

Ne sejte mi iznad groba cveće,
Rumen-ružu, mirisni bosiljak;
Već po grobu pelen zasadite,
Gorki pelen i oštru ostrugu:
Kad je ceo život pelen bio,
Našto će mi mrtvome bosiljak?
Kad je život prepun trnja bio,
Našto će mi posle smrti ruža?

Ne sejte mi iznad groba cveće,
Rumen-ružu, mirisni bosiljak;
Jer kad grane prvo premaleće,
Iz ruže će poniknut' ostruga,
Iz bosiljka pelen procvatiti:
Pelen će vam gorke suze mamit',
A ostruga srce razdirati,
Što mi niste zavet ispunili!

Velimir Rajić

Do not plant flowers on my grave,
Red roses and sweet smelling basil;
But plant wormwood on my grave,
Bitter wormwood and thorny brambles:
Since all my life is bitter wormwood
What good is basil to me dead?
Since all my life is filled with thorns
What good are roses after death?

Do not plant flowers on my grave,
Red roses and sweet smelling basil;
For when next spring appears
Red roses will turn to brambles
And basil turn to wormwood:
Wormwood will bring you bitter tears,
And brambles will tear at your heart,
For not fulfilling my dying wish.

Velimir Rajić

Milan RAKIĆ 1876 / 1938

Napuštena crkva

Leži stara slika raspetoga Hrista.
Mlaz mu krvi curi niz slomljena rebra;
Oči mrtve, usne blede, Samrt ista;
Nad glavom oreol od kovanog srebra.

Dar negdašnjeg plemstva i pobožnog sebra,
Djerdan od dukata o vratu mu blista;
Po okviru utisnuta srma čista,
A okvir je rez'o umetnik iz Debra.

Takav leži Hristos sred pustoga hrama.
I dok, postepeno, svuda pada tama,
I jato se noćnih tica na plen sprema,

Sam u pustoj crkvi, gde kruže vampiri,
Očajan i strašan, Hristos ruke širi,
Večno čekajući pastvu, koje nema...

Milan Rakić

The Abandoned Church

There lies the ancient icon of the crucified Christ.
A trickle of blood seeps down His broken ribs;
Eyes dead, lips pale, Death itself;
Above the head, a halo of hammered silver.

Donated by former nobles and pious serfs,
A necklace of ducats glows about His neck;
The icon's frame inlaid in pure silver,
Was chased by an artist from Debar.

Thus lies Christ within the barren temple,
As dusk gradually falls everywhere,
And a flight of night birds prepares for plunder,

Alone in the barren church where bats circle,
Desolate and awesome Christ opens His arms,
Eternally awaiting a flock that is no more...

Milan Rakić

Simonida

Iskopaše ti oči, lepa sliko!
Večeri jedne, na kamenoj ploči,
Znajuči da ga tad ne vidi niko,
Arbanas ti je nožem izbo oči.

Ali dirnuti rukom nije hteo
Ni otmeno ti lice, niti usta,
Ni zlatnu krunu, ni kraljevski veo,
Pod kojim leži kosa tvoja gusta.

I sad u crkvi, na kamenom stubu,
U iskićenom mozaik-odelu,
Dok mirno snosiš sudbu tvoju grubu,
Gledam te tužnu, svečanu i belu;

I kao zvezde ugašene, koje
Čoveku ipak šalju svetlost svoju,
Te čovek vidi sjaj, oblik i boju
Dalekih zvezda što već ne postoje,

Tako na mene, sa mračnoga zida,
Na počadjaloj i starinskoj ploči,
Sijaju sada, tužna Simonida,—
Tvoje već davno iskopane oči!

Milan Rakić

Simonida

Your eyes were gouged, beautiful image!
One night, on that slab of stone,
Confident no one would see him,
An Albanian with his knife gouged your eyes.

But he dared not touch his hand to
Your noble face, or your lips,
Your golden crown, or the regal veil
Beneath which lay your heavy hair.

Now, in this church, on a stone pillar
In your ornate mosaic robes,
While you calmly bear your cruel fate,
I watch you sad, solemn, and white;

Like stars burned out long ago,
Whose light shines on through space,
Bringing man the glow and shape and color,
Of remote stars no longer there,

So, for me, from this dark wall,
From this soot covered, ancient slab,
Still shine upon me, sad Simonida—
Your eyes gouged so long ago!

Milan Rakić

Kondir

Počuj, draga, reči iskrene i jasne
Jedne bolne duše, tvojoj duši prisne,
Pre no oluj stigne i grom strašni prasne,
I nemirno srce najedanput svisne,
Počuj ove pesme uzaludno strasne.

Pre odsudnog boja ja ti nisam dao
Koprenu, ni burmu, ni azdiju, kao
Starinski junaci, po čemu ćeš mene
Pomenuti kada stigne udes zao
I zapište deca i zaplaču žene.

Sad na razbojištu leži leš do leša.
Plemići i sebri. Leži strašna smeša.
Noć se hvata. Samo munja katkad blisne.
Dok poslednje žrtve stari krvnik veša,
Nepregledna hrpa ranjenika kisne...

Hoće li me naći medju njima tvoje
Bistre oči draga? Hoće l' iz kondira,
Ko preteča skromna večitoga mira,
Pasti kap na rane što zjape i gnoje?
Hoće l'pasti kaplja što bolove spira?

The Ewer

Listen, my love, to these words so sincere and pure,
Uttered by an anguished soul, so close to your own,
Before the storm descends and the fearsome thunder roars,
And a restless heart suddenly surrenders,
Listen to these poems passionate in vain.

Before the fatal combat I did not give you
A veil, or a wedding band, or a token
As did ancient heroes, something by which one day
You may remember me when evil strikes,
And children scream and women weep.

Now on the field the dead lie body by body,
Noblemen and serfs. Scattered in awesome confusion.
Night is falling. Now and then lightning flashes,
While the long-time foe hangs the last victims,
An endless mass of wounded lies drenched in the rain...

Shall I be found among them by your
Anxious eyes, my love? And will then from the ewer,
As a simple harbinger of eternal peace,
Fall water on wounds that fester and gape?
Will a drop fall to subdue the pain?

Čekam. Nigde nikog. Svetlost dana gasne.
Noć prosipa tamu i časove kasne,
Ni zvezde na nebu da za trenut blisne.
—Čekam. Nigde nikog. Uz vapaje glasne
Nepregledna hrpa ranjenika kisne...

Milan Rakić

I wait. No one in sight. The daylight fades.
Night pours forth darkness and late hours.
Not a star in the sky to shine for a moment.
—I wait. No one in sight. With intense cries
An endless mass of wounded lies drenched in the rain...

Milan Rakić

Orhideja

Kada sam te vid'o kraj mirisnih leja,
U parku, uz pesmu sakrivenih gnezda,
S viticama, s velom i, k'o crna zvezda,
Na belom šeširu crna orhideja,—

Tajanstveni suton, pun ljubavi strasne,
Šaptao je čeznju kroz mirisne grane;
Dok poslednja rumen na zapadu gasne,
I mir, mir svečani, pada na sve strane.

Ja za tobom idjah, i u jednom mahu,
Slušajući tice i talase rečne,
Ja osetih silno, u pobožnom strahu,
Da je najzad doš'o čas ljubavi večne,

Čas ljubavi prave, željene i čedne.
I sve što u duši mojoj beše časno,
I dobro, i nežno ispod kore ledne,
Prenu se, i živnu, i zaklikta glasno!

Ali ti ne rekoh ni "silno te ljubim"
Niti "dušo", niti "oči moje sjajne",
Niti praznom reči i pokretom grubim
Zbrisah čedne draži nekazane tajne;

The Orchid

When I saw you near the fragrant flower beds,
In the park, along with the song of hidden nests,
With your locks, your veil, and like a black star,
Upon your white hat, a large black orchid,—

The mysterious sunset, filled with passionate love,
Whispering longings through sweet scented boughs;
While in the west the pink color fades,
And peace, solemn peace, descends everywhere.

I walked behind you, and at that very moment,
Listening to the song of birds and river waves,
I felt intensely, steeped in religious fear,
That the moment of eternal love had arrived at last,

That moment of love, true, longed for, and virtuous.
And all that my soul held which was pure and honest,
And good, and tender, underneath the crust of ice,
Rose from slumber, began to live, and shout with joy!

I did not tell you then "I adore you,"
Nor did I say "my love," or "Sweetheart,"
Neither did I with senseless words or brutal gesture
Erase the virginal charm of an untold secret;

Jer k'o snežna lava, u istome času,
Survaše se na me bol, tuga, i strava,
Tajna strava koja u trenutku zasu
Klice nove nade i života prava.

I u čudnom strahu ja se pitah tada:
Kakvo sudba sprema ispaštanje veće,
I koliko treba nevolje i jada,
Da isplatim ovaj čas nenadne sreće!

I ne videh ništa. Ni daleke gore
Zabradjene tankim velom magle plave,
Ni ritove mnoge što spokojno gore
Kraj obala mirnih nepomične Save.

Ti prodje.—Uz pesmu sakrivenih gnezda,
I tajanstven šumor žbunova i leja,
Predznak duge bede, kao kobna zvezda,
Dizala se zlobna, crna orhideja.

Milan Rakić

For at that very moment, as an avalanche,
Descended upon me pain, sadness, and terror,
That secret terror which in one instant routed
The germs of new hopes and existing life.

And with deep fear I wondered in that brief instant:
What kind of deeper atonement fate bears,
And how much more misfortune and sorrow
Will come to pay for this unexpected bliss!

All became blurred. I saw not forests
Wrapped in their thin veil of bluish fog,
Nor the peaceful marshes shining serenely
Next to the still banks of the immobile Sava.

You walked by. — Along with the songs from hidden nests
And the mysterious murmur of boughs and flowers
As an omen of long grief, like a fateful star,
Rose the malicious, black orchid.

Milan Rakić

Ljubavna pesma

Šume bokori cvetnog jorgovana,
I noć zvezdana treperi, i žudi
Za bujnu ljubav, svetu Bogom dana.
Dok mesečina nasmejana bludi,
Šume bokori cvetnog jorgovana.

U taku noć je požudnu i strasnu
Izolda nekad čekala Tristana.
Bude se groblja uz kuknjavu glasnu,
I sećaju se prohujalih dana.
U taku noć je požudnu i strasnu,

Noseći sobom lestvice od svile,
Starinski vitez pun vere i nade,
Hitao zamku svoje verne Vile,
I pevao joj strasne serenade;
Starinski vitez pun vere i nade!

Šumi, o noći prohujalog doba!
U srcu nosim nekadanje ljude;
Povorke bele dižu se iz groba
I sa mnom ljube, čeznu, strepe, žude!
Šumi, o noći prohujalog doba,

A Love Poem

Large clusters of lilacs hum in full bloom,
The star studded night vibrates and yearns,
God gave it to the world for luxuriant love,
While smiling moonlight roams about,
Large clusters of lilacs hum in full bloom!

In such a lustful and passionate night
Isolde once waited for Tristan.
Graveyards awake with loud wailing,
Remembering days that have long since gone.
In such a lustful and passionate night,

Carrying with him a ladder made of silk,
An ancient knight filled with faith and hope,
Hurried to the castle of his faithful Lady,
And sang for her, passionate serenades;
An ancient knight filled with faith and hope!

Hum, oh night of times that are no more!
I carry in my heart men from former days;
While processions arise from their tombs
And with me, love, yearn, and fear, and long!
Hum, oh night of times that are no more,

Strasno i žudno! Ona mene čeka
K'o nekad plava Izolda Tristana.
Strepi, i sluša topot iz daleka...
Dok mesečina nasmejana sija,
I ćuv mirisni zanosno ćarlija
U bokorima cvetnog jorgovana.

Milan Rakić

Lustfully and passionately! She awaits me
As once the blond Isolde waited for Tristan.
Anxious, she listens for the thud of horse's hoofs...
While smiling moonlight shines all around
And fragrant breezes waft gently
In the clusters of lilacs in their full bloom

Milan Rakić

Serenada
(1-3)
1 Allegro

Sa tri svirača u crnome plaštu,
Sa šeširom na kom se pero vije,
Uzev u pomoć istočnjačku maštu,
Prikrašću se k'o lopov što se krije,
Sa tri svirača u crnome plaštu.

I zaječaće setne violine
U svežu noć kroz baštu cveća punu,
I kad kroz oblak bledi mesec sine
Poviće cveće svoju rosnu krunu,
I zaječaće setne violine.

O, to će biti silna pesma, rada
Da znaš šta nežna duša dragoj pruža;
Na moja usta pokuljaće tada
Milosne reči i bokori ruža.
Da, pesma moja biće moćna tada,

Pesma mladosti, burna kao ona,
Otmena, sveža, ponosna i vrela,
I silna kao mnogobrojna zvona
Kad proslavljaju pobednika smela!
Otmena, sveža, ponosna i vrela.

Serenade
(1-3)
1 Allegro

With three violin players in black capes,
With a hat upon which a feather hovers,
Aided by an oriental imagination,
I shall sneak like a thief hiding,
With three violin players in black capes.

And nostalgic violins will begin to sing
In the cool night, through the garden filled with blooms,
And when the pale moon breaks through clouds,
The flowers will bend their dew-covered crowns,
And nostalgic violins will begin to sing.

Oh, this will be a powerful song, eager
For you to know what a tender soul can offer;
From my lips will flow at that moment
Tender words like clusters of roses.
Yes, my song will be powerful at that moment,

A song of youth, tempestuous as youth itself,
Refined, refreshing, proud and passionate,
And powerful as are countless bells
When they celebrate a daring conqueror!
Refined, refreshing, proud and passionate.

O, kako će se zgranuti od čuda
Dremljive ćifte i njihove žene
Kad ih iz teškog, glupog sanka prene
Svemoćna pesma što prodire svuda!
O, kako će se zgranuti od čuda

Bednici jedni što nam ljubav krate,
Naviknuti na otrcane fraze,
Kojima lažu svoje tašte maze
Kasapski momci, kaplari, i ćate!
Bednici jedni što nam ljubav krate!

I zaječaće setne violine
U svežu noć, i staće pesma ova;
I kad, k'o potsmeh na tu sreću taštu,
Vesela zora na istoku sine,
Sa tri svirača u crnome plaštu
Poći ću—da ti sutra dodjem snova!

Milan Rakić

Oh, how taken aback by this miracle
Will be drowsy petty merchants and their wives,
When startled from their heavy stupid slumber
By this powerful song permeating all!
Oh, how taken aback by this miracle they will be

Those despicable people who deny us love,
Used as they are to the trite phrases
With which they flatter their vain spoiled darlings,
Butchers' boys, petty corporals and scribes!
Those despicable people who deny us love!

And nostalgic violins will begin to sing,
In the cool night; then this song will stop;
And when, as a mockery of our vain happiness,
A merry dawn breaks in the east,
With three violin players in black capes,
I shall leave—only to return tomorrow!

Milan Rakić

Iskrena pesma

O sklopi usne, ne govori, ćuti!
Ostavi dušu, nek' spokojno sneva—
Dok kraj nas lišće na drveću žuti,
I laste lete put toplih krajeva.

O sklopi usne, ne miči se, ćuti!
Ostavi misli, nek' se burno roje,
I reč nek' tvoja ničim ne pomuti
Bezmerno silne osećaje moje.

Ćuti, i pusti da sad žile moje
Zabrekću novim zanosnim životom,
Da zaboravim da smo tu nas dvoje
Pred veličanstvom prirode! A potom,

Kad prodje sve, i malaksalo telo
Ponovo padne u običnu čamu,
I život nov, i nadahnuće celo,
Nečujno, tiho, potone u tamu—

Ja ću ti, draga, opet reći tada
Otužnu pesmu o ljubavi, kako
Čeznem i stradam i ljubim te, ma da
U tom trenutku ne osećam tako...

A Sincere Poem

Oh, close your lips, do not speak, keep silent!
Leave the soul alone, let it dream in peace—
While around us leaves are turning on the trees,
And swallows are leaving for warmer skies.

Oh, close your lips, do not move, keep silent!
Leave my thoughts alone, let them swarm,
And let not your word in any way disturb
The infinite power of my emotions.

Keep silent and let my veins at this moment
Start to pound with a new and ravishing life,
Let me forget that there are two of us here
Facing the majesty of nature! Then later,

When all is over and the exhausted body
Falls back into the everyday tedium,
And the new life, and the whole inspiration,
Silently, calmly, sink back into darkness—

Then I shall tell you, dear, again and anew,
The insipid poem abut love, and how
I long for you, and suffer, and love, although
At that moment I shall not feel so...

A ti ćes, bedna ženo, kao vazda,
Slušati rado ove reči lažne:
I zahvalićeš Bogu što te sazda,
I oči će ti biti suzom vlažne.

I gledajući, vrh zaspalih njiva
Kako se spušta nema polutama,
Ti nećeš znati šta u meni biva,—
Da ja u tebi volim sebe sama,

I moju ljubav naspram tebe, kad me
Obuzme celog silom koju ima,
I svaki živac rastrese i nadme,
I osećaji navale k'o plima!

Za taj trenutak života i milja,
Kad zatreperi cela moja snaga,
Neka te srce moje blagosilja!
Al' ne volim te, ne volim te, draga.

I zato cu ti uvek reci: Cuti!
Ostavi dušu nek' spokojno sniva —
Dok kraj nas lišće na drvecu zuti,
I tama pada vrh zaspalih njiva.

Milan Rakić

And you, wretched woman, will as always
Listen gladly to all these false words:
And you will thank God for the life he gave you,
And tears will appear and make your eyes moist.

And watching over sleepy meadows, how slowly
Descends a quiet and silent twilight,
You will not understand my real emotion,—
That in you I love but myself.

And that this love I feel for you, when
It grasps me with all the power it has,
And makes each nerve tremble with new life and vigor,
While feelings gush like a high tide!

For that instant of life and delight,
When I sense the trembling of my entire being,
For that, let my whole heart bless you!
But I don't love you, I don't love you, dear!

That is why I shall always say: keep silent!
Leave the soul alone, let it dream in peace—
While around us leaves are turning on the trees,
And darkness descends over sleeping fields.

Milan Rakić

Obična pesma

Naša je ljubav bila kratkog veka,
Trenutak jedan—tek godinu dana.
I rastavi nas naglo sudba preka,
Bez uzdisaja, bez suza, bez rana.

U svadji nam je prošlo pola dana;
U pomirenju mučnom pola noći.
I bežao sam iz našega stana,
Tražeći mira u poljskoj samoći.

No to je bilo samo kratko vreme;
Pa postadosmo tudji jedno drugom;
I gledasmo se u ćutanju dugom,
Tupo, k'o sito dete šećerleme.

I tako sve je prošlo; i ja sada
Ne mogu kleti nebo ni sudbinu,
Il' s pesnicama stisnutim, pun jada,
Prokleti žene ili podlost njinu!

Pa ipak—da si samo katkad znala
Veliki, kobni oganj duše ove,
I silnu ljubav što ništi k'o hala
Sve druge misli i nade i snove;—

A Plain Poem

Our love was brief, and so short-lived,
Barely a moment—merely a year.
And cruel fate separated us swiftly,
Without a sigh, a tear, a wound.

Half our days we spent in bitter strife;
Half our nights in painful reconciliation,
And I had to flee from our dwelling
And seek peace in the loneliness of fields.

And that, too, was only for a short time;
And then we became completely estranged;
And we stared at each other in endless silence,
Bored, like a child tired of too many sweets.

And so all was over; and at present
I cannot curse heaven or my own fate,
Nor can I with clenched fists, in pain,
Curse all women and their malicious baseness!

But with all that—had you ever fathomed
The great, fatal fire burning in this soul,
This powerful love which destroys like a dragon
All other thoughts, or hopes, or dreams;—

Pa ipak—da si samo katkad htela
U zanosu, i sličnu mekoj svili,
Da kažeš nežnu reč iz srca vrela—
I mi bi možda dugo srećni bili!

A sad polako teče ovo vreme;
Postasmo tako tudji jedno drugom;
I gledamo se u ćutanju dugom
Tupo, k'o sito dete šećerleme.

Milan Rakić

But, with all that—had you ever deigned
In a moment of fervor, akin to soft silk,
To utter a tender word from a passionate heart—
We might have been happy for a long time!

And now time crawls so slowly for us,
We have become completely estranged,
And we stare at each other in endless silence,
Bored, like a child tired of too many sweets.

Milan Rakić

U kvrgama

U kvrge su me bacili, o srama!
Da, to je bilo u prastaro vreme.
Jesam li bio kriv? i zašto? Tama
Ćuti, i redom sva stvorenja neme.
U kvrge su me bacili, o srama!

Neko ih steže, a ne vidim ko je!
Al' čujem kako škripe kvrge gnusne.
Pod silnom stegom peršte kosti moje,
I krv iz rana na mahove pljusne.
Neko ih steže, a ne vidim ko je!

Jauk i piska svuda oko mene!
U redovima crnim kvrge stoje;
U njima pište deca, ljudi, žene.
Neko ih muči, a ne znaju ko je.
Jauk i piska svuda oko mene!

Steži, o steži nevidljiva silo!
I nemilosno kosti moje mrvi;
Dok najzad moje ne prestane bilo,
I ne iscuri kap poslednje krvi!
Steži, o steži, nevidljiva silo!

In Irons

I was put in irons, oh shame!
Yes, it happened in days long gone by.
Was I guilty? And of what? The darkness
Is silent and all beings are mute.
I was put in irons, oh shame!

Someone turns the screws, but I see not who!
Though I hear the grinding of the loathsome irons.
Under their forceful grip my bones are crushed,
And from time to time my blood gushes forth.
Someone tightens the screws, but I see not who!

Moans and shrieks resound all around me!
In long, black rows the irons are set,
In them wail men, women, and children.
Someone is torturing them, but they know not who!
Moans and shrieks resound all around me!

Turn, oh turn the screws, you invisible power!
And crush my bones without the slightest pity,
Until at last my heart stops beating,
And the last drop of my blood is drained!
Turn, oh turn the screws, you invisible power!

O, kako ti se slatko smejem sada!
Žrtva se ruga dželatu što kolje.
Zar to vrhunac mučenja i jada?
Zar ništa nisi izmislila bolje?
O, kako ti se slatko smejem sada!

Udri, i muči, i priteži jače—
Al' znaj de neće preći moje usne
Ni jedna reč'ca što moli il' plače,
Ni bapske kletve, ni slabosti gnusne!
Udri i muči, i priteži jače!

Al' dokle redom deca, ljudi, žene,
Plaču i pište, bedni, pokraj mene,
I ropski kleče pred skrivenim stvorem,
Vrh piske, kletve, i vapaja njini'
Leteće mirno duh moj u visini,
K'o morska lasta nad širokim morem!

Milan Rakić

Oh, with what relish I laugh at you now!
The victim mocks the torturer who slays.
Is this the peak of pain and agony?
Is there nothing better you could have found?
Oh, with what relish I laugh at you now!

Strike, and torture, and turn the screws tighter—
But know that never will you hear from my lips
Escape a word of lament or an appeal for mercy,
Or old women curses, or repulsive weakness!
Strike, and torture, and turn the screws tighter!

But while men, women and children
Cry out, and moan, crushed all around me,
Kneel like slaves at the feet of the hidden being,
Above their shrieks, their curses, and wailings,
My spirit will soar, calm, into the heights,
Like a sea swallow over high seas.

Milan Rakić

Želja

Kad i meni dodje čas da mreti treba,
Bože, daj da umrem u jesenje noći,
Nasmejan i vedar u mladačkoj moći,
Pod raskošnim sjajem septembarskog neba!

Smrt je tako laka. Al' pratilja njena,
Sva taština što se pred smrt snova budi,
I zanatske suze zabradjenih žena,
I bol izveštačen ravnodušnih ljudi,

I mantije crne, čiraci i čoja—
Sve to tako grubo i surovo dira,
I gnusobom vredja osećanja moja,
Pred skromnom lepotom večitoga mira!

O, umreti tako! bez piske, bez sveta,
Bez dosadne, glupe komedije smrti,
Nečujno k'o miris uvenulog cveta;
I život i dugo očajanje smrti,

Kao jednim dahom, u mladačkoj moći,
Pod raskošnim sjajem septembarske noći!

A Wish

When for me, too, comes the time to die,
Lord, allow me to die during autumn nights,
Smiling and serene in the power of youth,
Under the sumptuous splendor of a September sky!

Death is so easy. But all her retinue,
All the vanity that wakens at her approach,
The expected tears of women in black kerchiefs,
And the artificial grief of indifferent men,

All the black robes of priests, all the candles and mourning—
All this hurts in so crude and cruel a way,
And this filth of death insults my emotions,
In front of the modest beauty of eternal rest!

Oh, to die so! Without screaming or people,
Without the dull, stupid comedy of dying,
Inaudible as dies the scent of a wilting flower;
And to erase life and all endless despair,

All this in one breath, in the power of youth,
Under the sumptuous splendor of a September sky!

Ti bi došla k meni bez suze u oku,
I ako te boli razdiru i guše,
Skrivajući jade i tugu duboku
U kutima tajnim nežne tvoje duše.

Ti bi došla k meni, i pogledom jednim
Poslednje bi zbogom rekla starom drugu,
I miloštom krasnom, i poljupcem čednim,
Zbrisala bi tajnu, neizbežnu tugu.

Dodji! Čas je kucn'o! K'o u srećne dane,
Poći ćemo sami iz dosadnog grada,
Poći ćemo sami u pitome strane,
Daleko od ljudi, daleko od jada.

O hajd'mo u svetlost, u polja, u cveće,
U čednu tišinu uspavane noći,
U miloštu tajnu što iz zvezda sleće,
I svečano struji po vedroj samoći!

Gledaj kako mesec nad poljima sija,
I oblake retke rastura i vedri,
I trava miriše, i rastinje klija,
I šumore tužno kukuruzi jedri!

Nad nama će nebo treptati u sjaju,
Grliće nas blago vaseljena nema,
Lepršnuće krilom u obližnjem gaju
Slepi miš poslednji što se na put sprema.

Pa dok iz daljine grmi gradska jeka,
I zabave puste što nize čoveka,
I bučno veselje tajanstveno huji,
Zapevaće negde skriveni slavuji—

You would come to me without a tear in your eye,
Though choked and torn apart with suffering,
You would hide your sorrow and your endless sadness
In the secret corners of your tender soul.

You would come to me, and with only one look
You would say a last farewell to an old companion,
And with loving tenderness, and a modest kiss,
Erase the secret, inevitable sadness.

Come! The time is now! As during happy days,
We shall go alone from the boring city,
We shall go alone to the pleasant regions,
Far away from people, far away from sorrows.

Oh, let us go toward light, and fields, and flowers,
Into the virtuous silence of the sleepy night,
Into the secret tenderness that falls from the stars,
And flows so festively in the serene solitude!

Look how the moonlight flows all over the fields,
And chases scarce clouds and clears the sky,
And the grass is scented, and all plants sprout,
And how sadly rustles the overripe corn!

Above us the sky will twinkle with splendor,
And the soundless universe will embrace us softly,
And in a neighboring glen will flutter
The last bat ready for its nocturnal flight.

Then, while from the distance thunders the city bustle,
With senseless amusements that belittle men,
And loud celebrations that mysteriously throb,
Hidden somewhere nightingales will start singing—

I priroda cela zašumeće strasno,
I polja, i gore, i bašte, i vrti—
Sve što u njoj živi pozdraviće glasno
Svečani dolazak ravnodušne smrti.

Zaćutaću tada. Nema reči više,
Poljubiću samo tvoju ruku bledu;
I dišući mirno, sve tiše i tiše,
Ostaviću život, nevolju i bedu,
Bezbrižan i vedar, nasmejan i čio.

I sklopicu oči za navek! I tada,
Osetiću čudno, kao kad se sniva,
Sa miloštom tajnom što iz zvezda pada,
I svežinom skoro pooranih njiva,
Sjaj očiju tvojih bolećiv i mio.

Milan Rakić

And all nature will hum with passion,
Fields and forests, and gardens, and blossoms—
All that lives in nature will greet aloud
The solemn arrival of the indifferent death.

Then I shall become silent, there are no more words,
All I will do is kiss your pale hand;
And breathing calmly, always more and more quietly,
I shall depart from life, from sorrows and grief,
Carefree and serene, vigorous and smiling,

And close my eyes forever! And then,
Mysteriously I shall feel as in a dream,
With the secret tenderness that falls from the stars,
And the freshness that rises from recently plowed fields,
The light of your eyes, so compassionate and loving.

Milan Rakić

Jovan DUČIĆ   1871 / 1943

Moja poezija

Mirna kao mramor, hladna kao sena,
Ti si bledo, tiho devojče što sneva.
Pusti pesma drugih neka bude žena
Što po nečistijem ulicama peva.

Ja ne mećem na te djindjuve sa trakom,
Nego žute ruže u te kose duge:
Budi odveć lepa da se svidjaš svakom,
Odveć gorda da bi živela za druge.

Budi odveć tužna sa sopstvenih jada
Da bi išla ikad da tešiš ko strada,
A čedna da vodiš gomile što nagle.

I stoj ravnodušna, dok oko tvog tela,
Mesto kitnjastog i raskošnog odela,
Lebdi samo pramen tajanstvene magle.

Jovan Dučić

My Poetry

Peaceful as marble, cold as a wraith,
You are a pale, calm maiden adreaming.
Let the poetry of others be like a woman
Filling unclean streets with her songs.

I adorn you not with cheap beads and ribbons,
Instead, yellow roses I braid in your hair:
Be too lovely to be pleasing to all,
And too proud to live your life for others.

Be too wistful with your own sorrows
Ever to stir to console those who suffer,
Too pure to lead rushing, thoughtless crowds.

And stand there aloof, while around your body,
Instead of an ornate and luxuriant robe,
Floats only a strand of mysterious mist.

Jovan Dučić

Sunce

Rodio se na Jonskom Moru, na obalama punim sunca, tamnih vrtova, i bledih statua, i, kao galeb, okupao se u azuru, svetlosti, i mirisu večito zagrejanih voda. Majka ga je često nosila po studenim senkama nekog drveća čije je lišće mirisalo mirisom sna. Nesrećni pesnik! Detetom je otišao u kraj gde je nebo bledo i smrzlo, na kome gori bledo i hladno sunce, i po čijim obalama plaču vetrovi. I jedna misao, kao rana, opominjala ga je večito na njegovu sunčanu obalu, tamne vrtove, i mirne statue. I zajedno s talasima i vetrovima, on je plakao gorko i neutešno na žalovima melanholičnog tudjeg mora.

Ali kada su njegove kose, plave kao uvelo lišće, postale bele; kada su njegove strasne i lepe oči, koje su nekad imale boju zimskog limunovog granja ili plitkog mora, postale mutne; kada je u svojim venama osetio zimu koja nema svog proleća, Usud ga je vratio ponovo u Joniju.

Sve je tamo bilo kao i pre. Ali *on* ne beše više onaj isti; i sunčane obale veselog i strasnog Jonskog Mora nije mogao da pozna! Bolno, on stište oči i pogleda u se. I, gle! tamo, on vide ono nekadanje sunce, ono čudno i ogromno sunce, što činjaše nekada da sve oko njega živi, da lišće ima miris sna, i da vidi belu i hladnu krv statua gde struji kroz mirni kamen, i čini da i on živi i pati dubokom i silnom strašću ljudi.

To je bilo Sunce Mladosti što je minula, sunce što je svetlilo još samo duboko u večernjem sutonu jedne duše, i

The Sun

He was born on the shores of the Ionean Sea, on shores filled with sunlight, dark gardens, and pale statues, and like a seagull, he bathed in the azure, the light, and the fragrance of perpetually warm waters. His mother carried him often through the cool shadows of trees with leaves which were scented with the fragrance of dreams.

Poor poet! As a child he left for regions where the sky was pallid and frozen, and where the sun burned white and cold, and along the shores of which winds wailed. And one thought, like a wound, reminded him constantly of his sunny shores, of his dark gardens, and serene statues. With the waves and the winds he wept, bitter and disconsolate, on the shores of a melancholy foreign sea.

But when his hair, blond as dry leaves, turned white, when his beautiful and passionate eyes which once were the color of boughs on lemon trees in winter or of the shallow sea became dull, when he felt in his veins a winter that has no spring, Fate brought him back to the Ionean Sea.

Everything was the same as it had been before. But *he* was not the same and he did not recognize the sunny shores of the joyous and passionate Ionean Sea! Grieving, he closed his eyes and gazed deeply into himself. And there! there he saw that same sun of the past, that strange and enormous sun which gave life to all things around him and the fragrance of dreams to the leaves, and made him see the white and cold koje je davalo svemu što je obasjavalo čudnu i magijsku lepotu Iluzije.

Jer stvari imaju onakav izgled kakav im dadne naša duša.

Jovan Dučić

blood flow through the serene stone of statues, and made him live and suffer with the deep and powerful passions of men.

It was the Sun of Youth that had passed, a sun which alone enlightened the depth and twilight of his soul, and which bestowed upon all it illuminated the strange and magic beauty of Illusion.

For things appear as the soul perceives them.

Jovan Dučić

Mala princeza

Mala princeza, čije su kose imale boju mesečeve svet-losti, čiji je pogled bio modar, i čiji je glas imao miris žutih ruža,—mala princeza je umorna od života, i ona je tužna.

Ona je na svojim širokim mramornim teracama nad morem, pored ogromnih vaza u kojima su mirno umirale njezine krizanteme, plakala kradomice u duge mutne večeri. Njena nostalgija i neizvesna tuga umarale su njenu krv i telo, koji su bili onaki isti kao krv i telo u ljiljana.

I u tople noći, kada je vazduh pun zlatne zvezdane pra-šine, I dok na mračnim zidovima spavaju mirni paunovi, i kada svi cvetovi otvaraju svoja srca, otvaralo se i srce male princeze. Zato su te noći bile tako pune tuge i toplote.

A kada je umrla, nečujno i spokojno kao što su poumi-rale njezine krizanteme, dugo su sa katedrale pevala stara zvona, a glasovi tih zvona bili su mirni i svečani kao glasovi davno pomrlih sveštenika.

Jovan Dučić

The Little Princess

The little princess whose hair was the color of moonlight, whose eyes were deep blue and whose voice had the fragrance of yellow roses—the little princess was weary of life and she was sad.

On the large marble terraces overlooking the sea, next to the enormous vases in which her chrysanthemums were dying peacefully, she wept in secret during long, vague evenings. A mysterious nostalgia and an unknown sadness exhausted her blood and her body, which were the blood and the body of a lily.

And during warm nights when the air was filled with the gold dust of stars, and white serene peacocks were asleep on dark walls, and when all flowers opened their hearts, the heart of the little princess opened as well. So were these nights filled with sadness and warmth.

And when she died as suddenly and as peacefully as her chrysanthemums, the ancient bells from the cathedral tolled for a long time, and the sounds of the bells were as peaceful and as solemn as the voices of long dead priests.

Jovan Dučić

Morska vrba

Sama vrba stoji nad morem na steni,
Rasplela je kosu zelenu i dugu:
Naliči na nimfu koju su prokleli
Da postane drvo i da šumi tugu.

Sluša pesmu gora kada jutro rudi,
Agoniju vode u večeri neme;
Nepomično stoji tamo gde sve bludi:
Oblaci i vetri, talasi i vreme.

I tu šumi s njima, dajući polako,
Moru koju granu, vetru listak koji;
I, k'o srce, sebe kidajući tako,
Tužno šumi život.—Sama vrba stoji...

Jovan Dučić

The Sea Willow

Alone stands the willow on a rock above the sea;
Her unbraided hair, long and green,
Resembling a nymph who was cursed
To become a tree and to hum with sorrow.

She listens to the chant of forests at daybreak,
To the agony of waters during mute twilight;
Motionless she stands among all things that roam:
Clouds and wind, waves and time.

And there she hums with them, slowly giving
A twig to the sea, a small leaf to the wind;
And akin to a heart tearing itself apart
Sadly she hums about life.—Alone stands the willow.

Jovan Dučić

*   *   *

Pustinja leži duga, i široka—
Veče, sja zapad...sve bukti u bl'jesku...
Al' na njoj nikog—samo razasuti
Skeleti neki vide se na p'jesku.

Tako zasv'jetli i u ljudskoj duši,
I vedra mis'o raspe svjetlost tajnu;
Al' često nema da ozari ništa,
Sem jedno groblje i pustoš beskrajnu...

Jovan Dučić

*   *   *

The desert stretches long and wide—
Twilight, the west glows...all ablaze in a flash...
But upon it, no one—only scattered
Skeletons exposed upon the sand.

Thus a man's soul lights up in a flash,
And a cheerful thought spreads its secret light;
Though it often has nothing to illuminate
But a graveyard and an endless wasteland.

Jovan Dučić

Sat

Dan bolestan, mutan, nebo neprozirno.
Nad bezbojnom vodom mir večernji beše.
Časovnik nevidljiv negde izbi mirno;
Tad potonje ruže lagano pomreše.

I kad opet izbi—s topola se rasu
Zadnje mrtvo lišće. Mir je na sve strane.
Dok ponova kucnu; tiho u tom času
Jedno gnezdo pade visoko sa grane...

No skriveno zvono kad pod svodom lednim
I opet se začu iz topola stari',
Sva dolina strahom ispuni se jednim,
I užasnom strepnjom, i panikom stvari.

Jovan Dučić

The Clock

The day was ill, turbid, under an opaque sky.
Over colorless waters lay the evening peace.
Somewhere an unseen clock chimed serenely;
While slowly the last roses continued to die.

And when the clock chimed anew—from the poplars
Fell the last wilted leaves. Peace everywhere.
Until the clock chimed again: then without a sound
A nest fell from high above a branch...

But, when under frozen skies, the hidden bell
Chimed again amidst the poplar trees,
The entire valley filled with an all consuming fear,
An overwhelming anxiety, and the panic of all things.

Jovan Dučić

Jablanovi

Zašto noćas tako šume jablanovi,
Tako strasno, čudno? Zašto tako šume?
Žut je mesec davno zašao za hume,
Daleke i crne k'o slutnje; i snovi

U toj mrtvoj noći pali su na vodu,
Ko olovo mirnu i sivu, u mraku.
Jablanovi samo visoko u zraku
Šume, šume čudno, i drkću u svodu.

...Sam kraj mirne vode, u noći, ja stojim,
K'o potonji čovek. Zemljom, prema meni,
Leži moja senka. Ja se noćas bojim
Sebe, i ja strepim sâm od svoje seni.

Jovan Dučić

The Poplars

Why do the poplars hum tonight in such a way,
Such a passionate and strange way? Why do they hum so?
The yellow moon descended long ago behind the hills
That were distant and dark as omens; and dreams

In that dead of night fell upon the waters
Which were calm and grey as lead in the darkness.
Only poplars high above in the air
Hummed, hummed strangely, and trembled against the sky.

...Alone, at the brink of tranquil waters, in the night, I stand,
As if the last man. On the ground, facing me,
Lies my shadow. Tonight I am afraid
Of myself, and I fear my own shadow.

Jovan Dučić

Poznanstvo

Kad sam je pozn'o, nebo beše mutno,
Zadnje su ruže umirale ti'o,
Jesenje vode šumljahu zloslutno;
I ja sam sniv'o, i tužan sam bio.

I moja mladost nije više znala
Za vedre strasti i čeznuća njina;
U moju dušu njena sen je pala;
Bleda i mrtva kao mesečina;

Ili k'o svetlost što u katedrali,
Po zidovima s kojih kaplje voda,
Kroz raznobojna okna, kao vali,
Prospe se hladna sa jesenjeg svoda.

Glas njezin beše k'o muzika tuge...
I za to mišljah, u slušanju mnogom,
Samo na prošlost, na jeseni duge,
Na hladno nebo, i na tužno, "zbogom."

Poljubac njezin beše tih i leden
Mramorni poljub; a kosa joj plava
Odisala je setan miris jedan
Bokora ruža koji docvetava.

The Acquaintanceship

When I first saw her, the sky was a dull grey,
And the last roses were dying quietly.
Autumnal waters murmured as an ill omen;
I was daydreaming and was melancholy.

Since that moment my youth lost all knowledge
Of cheerful passions and of all longings;
Into my soul fell the shadow of her being;
As pale and as dead as a moonlight beam;

Or as a light which through a vast cathedral,
Over thick walls from which water oozes,
Through multicolored panes akin to waves
Falls cold as if from an autumnal vault.

Her voice was like the music of sadness...
That is why I thought, while listening often,
Only about past days, and of endless autumns,
Of a cold sky, and of a sad "goodbye".

Her kiss was so calm and at the same time cold
As ice-cold marble; while her blond hair
Emitted the melancholy fragrance
Of a rose bush covered with wilting flowers.

I mnogo puta, kad u jutro sivo
Trgnem se iz sna—k'o iz teških uza,
I k'o iz olova—koji me pokrivo—
Oči mi behu mutne, pune suza.

Jovan Dučić

And so many times, while in a grey morning
I rose from sleep—as from heavy chains,
Or from beneath a lead sheet—which covered me—
My eyes were clouded and were filled with tears.

Jovan Dučić

Susret

Čekasmo se dugo, a kad smo se sreli
Dala si mi ruku i pošla si sa mnom.
I idući stazom nejasnom i tamnom,
Iskali smo sunca i sreće smo hteli.

Oboje smo strasno verovali tada
Da se besmo našli. I mi nismo znali
Koliko smo bili umorni i pali
Od jada, od davno preživljenih jada.

I za navek kad se rastasmo, i tako
Stežuc' svoje srce rukama obema,
Otišla si plačna, zamrzla i nema,
K'o što beše došla, tužno i polako.

Jovan Dučić

The Meeting

We waited long to meet, but when we did meet
You gave me your hand and we left together.
And following a path which was blurred and dim,
We sought sunshine and wanted happiness.

We both passionately believed at that moment
We had found each other. And we did not know
How tired we were and how defeated
By sorrows, by sorrows endured long ago.

And when forever we parted, in this way,
Pressing your heart with both your hands,
You left tearful, benumbed, without a word,
Just as you came, slowly, filled with sadness.

Jovan Dučić

Suton

Ja te volim jednim žarom neveselim
I sumnjom u tugu i lepotu jada:
Sreća koju imam uništava sada
Beskonačnu drugu sreću koju želim.

Zaklanjaš mi sunce, a dala si sama
Sto očiju mome srcu, i sve pute
Duši, da bi ipak sva nestala u te,
Kao izgubljeni zvuk u dolinama;

I sto volja kao belih jata k jugu,
Da sva na tvoj ostrv padnu očarana;
I sto vera da ti slede jednog dana,
Ko sto bele dece u litiju dugu.

Digla si sto mržnja, da stražare kao
Sto crnih jedrila, sva pred tvojom lukom;
I tako mom duhu prinela si rukom
Cvet tvog bića krupan, otrovan i zao.

I svom strašću prve i poslednje žene,
Vladaš mojom dušom, svom i svagda;—slična
Sudbi, tako i ti, silna, nepomična
Stojiš izmedj' mene i sveg oko mene;—

Twilight

I love you with a melancholy ardor
And with doubt in the beauty and gloom of sorrow:
The present happiness is destroying
The infinite other happiness I crave.

For me you erase sunshine, though you did give
A hundred eyes to my heart, and opened
New roads to my soul, but you had them all merge
In you, like sounds that fade into a valley!

A hundred desires resembling white flocks
Headed south, only to land bewitched on your isle;
A hundred religions to trail one day behind you
Like a hundred white-clad children in a procession.

You raised a hundred hatreds to stand guard
Like a hundred black sails at the entrance to your port;
Thus, to my soul you extended your hand
With the huge poisoned blossom of your being.

With all the passion of the first and last woman
You rule my soul, entire, forever—like
Fate, you too, reign omnipotent, immobile.
You stand between me and all that is around—

Dok iz suhe stene bije nova voda,
I plavi cvetovi iz staroga panja,
I sijaju kao u sam dan postanja
Sva zvezdana kola sa velikog svoda!

Moju ljubav, tamnu kao mrak u česti,
Ja ispunih mržnjom, kajanjem i strahom—
No žedj za izdajstvom pretvori se mahom
Sva u novi zavet i slast ispovesti.

Tako gorko pada neko veče bledo
Na sve moje pute; bolno, po sve doba,
Duboko u meni dok ljubav i zloba
Kao dva andjela poju naporedo.

Jovan Dučić

While from dried up rocks spring new waters,
And blue flowers blossom from an old stump,
And sparkle as on the day of their birth
All galaxies from a boundless sky!

My love, like the shadows in a thicket,
I filled with hatred, remorse and fear—
But my thirst for treason changed in a flash
Into new oaths and the delights of confession.

Thus falls bitterly, a certain faded twilight
Befogging my road; painfully and forever,
While deep in me, love and envious malice
Sing together like two angels in a choir.

Jovan Dučić

De Profundis

Ti utehu čekaš. Ne, utehe nema;
Što utehom zovu, zovi zaboravom;
Jad istinski dubok nikad ne zadrema.

Rastrzana tako medju snom i javom,
Gledajući kako nepomično bdije
Taj Andj'o Stradanja nad tužnom ti glavom.

Ti želiš i čekaš. I ne znaš da nije
Ni sad ispijena ta čemerna čaša,
I svirepi otrov jedne ironije;

I da će nas večno strašna prošlost naša
U nemirne noći da trgne i seti,
Kao zveket lanca starog robijaša.

Surovi će dani doći i uzeti
Svaki po svoj deo od srca što bunca,
Što želi, što moli; a ti ćeš se peti,

Peti neprekidno do kobnog vrhunca,
Golom stopom, bleda, smrzla, jadno dete,
Pružajuci ruke i vapijuć': Sunca!

De Profundis

You wait for solace. No, there is no solace;
What others call solace, you call oblivion;
A real, deep sorrow never falls asleep.

Thus, torn apart between vigilance and sleep,
Seeing and watching at your side the vigil
Of that Angel of sorrow that stands at your head,

You long and you wait. And you do not know
That the bitter chalice is not yet drained,
With its heartless poison of irony;

And eternally the horror of our past
Will haunt and remind us during listless nights,
As an old convict is reminded by the clicking of his chains.

Cruel days will come and each in turn will
Snatch its share of the heart that raves,
That longs and prays, while you keep ascending,

Ascending ceaselessly to the fateful peak,
Barefoot pale, frozen, pitiful child,
Spreading out your hands and begging for: Sun!

I tako ti dani bez sreće i mete,
Odnoseć' svoj deo stradanja i suza,
Kao gavrani će kraj nas da prolete,

I ne pokidavši ni jednu od uza
Što nas vežu i sad za prošlost, što stoji
Za nama i gleda na nas k'o Meduza.

Jovan Dučić

And thus, these days without happiness or goal,
Taking with them their share of sorrows and tears,
Like a flight of ravens, will fly by us,

Without breaking even one single tie
That binds us still, now, to the past which stands
Behind us, watching us, like Medusa.

Jovan Dučić

Dubrovački madrigal

Večeras, Gospodjo, u kneza na balu,
Igraćemo opet burni vals k'o prije;
S radošću na licu minućemo salu,
Kao da nikad ništa bilo nije!

A zatim će doći veseli kadrili,
Muzika će strasna da huji k'o bura;
Gospodje će biti u mletačkoj svili,
Gospoda u ruhu od crnog velura.

Zatim će vlastela u zbore da tonu!
Mladji o junaštvu, pesništvu i vinu,
Stariji o nebu, o starom Platonu,
I o skolastici, Svetom Avgustinu.

Mi ćemo, medjutim, sesti u dnu sale,
U meke fotelje, ne slušajuć' tezu,
I napisaću vam, hitro, k'o od šale,
Jedan tužan sonet na vašu lepezu.

Jovan Dučić

Madrigal from Dubrovnik

Tonight, My Lady, at the ball of the Doge,
We shall dance the whirling waltz as we once did;
With joyous faces we shall circle the ballroom,
As if nothing ever happened before.

Then merry quadrilles will follow,
Passionate music will swell like a storm;
Ladies will wear pure silk from Venice,
While gentlemen will dress in black velour.

In time, noblemen will drift into deliberation!
The young will speak of courage, poems, and wine,
The old, of heaven, and of ancient Plato,
Of Scholasticism, and of Saint Augustine.

Meanwhile, we shall sit at the far end of the hall,
In soft armchairs, not listening to their discourse,
And I shall jot rapidly as if it were a joke,
A very sad sonnet and inscribe it on your fan.

Jovan Dučić

Dubrovački poklisar

Zimi tisuć šesto...(sad svejedno koje),
Menčetić, poklisar, beše u Versalju,
Da učini smerno podvorenje svoje
Luju Četrnajstom, milostivom kralju.

U čast poslanika Republike stare,
I svetloga gosta, držali su bili
Tad u Trianonu briljantno soare,
S trupom Molijera, muzikom od Lili.

Svu noć napudrane markizice male,
Na vrh cipelica satinskih i finih,
Igrahu menuet; i miris duž sale
Vejaše k'o vetar od lepeza njinih;—

Dok je gost medjutim, prešao u zboru
S jednim kardinalom, pun rečite sile,
Celo stanje crkve na Jadranskom Moru,
Sve misleć' na jednu cipelu od svile.

Jovan Dučić

The Envoy from Dubrovnik

In a winter of the 1600s...(it matters not which)
Mencetic, the envoy, was at Versailles,
To present his humble respects
To Louis XIV, the almighty king.

To honor this envoy of the ancient Republic,
This distinguished guest, the court attended
A brilliant soiree in the Trianon
With the company of Molière, the music of Lully.

All night long dainty marquises with powdered hair
Danced the minuet on the tips of their tiny,
Refined satin slippers. Across the ballroom, perfume
Wafted on the drafts from their fans.

The guest, meanwhile, pondering in a discussion
With a cardinal inflated by eloquence,
The state of the Church on the Adriatic,
Was thinking only of a small, satin slipper.

Jovan Dučić

Dubrovačko vino

More nepomično, mirno kao srma,
Ležaše pred vrtom. Samo mlaz fontana
Prska. Dok iz modrog lavorovog grma
Viri bludno lice mramornoga Pana.

Ču se strasna svirka. Zatim društvo celo
Javi se u vrtu; sva su lica njina
Bila razdragana; sve beše veselo
Posle dobrog ručka i perfidnog vina.

I počeše igre, sve s nežnim darmarom;
Izvesna pometnja nastupi u činu:
Tu kapetan psalme citira sa žarom,
A dominikanac svira mandolinu:—

Gospodjica Ana de Doce, već seda,
Čuvena sa svojih strogih vrlina i tona,
Okružena jatom dama, pripoveda,
Jednu gromku priču iz "Dekamerona".

Jovan Dučić

Dubrovnik's Wine

The sea, immobile, mellow as old silver,
Stretched before the garden. Trickling waters
Splashed in the fountains. From the purple myrrh,
Peered the lusting face of a marble Pan.

Passionate music resounds. Company
Appears in the garden; each face
Aglow with gaiety; everything made merry
From sumptuous food and perfidious wine.

When time arrives for old games, a shiver of
Confusion surfaces in their actions.
There a Captain quotes church psalms with fervor
While a Dominican friar plays the mandolin.

The venerable Anna de Dozze, white-haired,
And famous for her exacting virtue and poise,
Surrounded by a bevy of ladies, tells
A droll tale straight from the *Decameron*.

Jovan Dučić

Dubrovački epitaf

Ova stara kuća sa grbom starinskim,
S balkonom na Stradun, gde mirišu sade
Godine i trulež hodnicima niskim,
Beše nekad kuća kneza Paska Zade.

Pasko Zade beše alhemicar; dalje,
Poznat pitagorist, zvezdar, moreplovac;
Djak slavnog Vanini.—Pučanin, sin švalje,
Posta plemić umom, a knezom za novac.

Letopisi kažu:—Beše mudrost sama...
Sto godina življe za muze i pare...
No slast ženskog tela ne pozna: od srama
Umre...sed k'o ovca, malen kao jare...

Epitaf: "Tu leži Pasko Zade, mili
Knez...(i tako dalje), uspomene jasne!
Jedini od ljudi s kim su uvek bili
Svi muževi dobri i sve žene časne."

Jovan Dučić

Epitaph in Dubrovnik

This old house with an ancient coat of arms
And a balcony on the Stradun, where the low
Corridors now smell of the past and decay,
Was once, long ago, the house of Prince Pasko Zade.

Pasko Zade was an alchemist, and more,
A well-known Pythagorist, astronomer, navigator;
A student of the famous Vanini.—Plebeian son of a seamstress,
He became a noble through thought and a prince through
  money.

Old chronicles state:—He was pure wisdom...
Lived a hundred years for Muses and money...
But never knew the delights of a woman's body: from shame
He died...white as an old sheep and small as a lamb...

Epitaph: "Here rests Pasko Zade, the beloved
Prince...(and so on) of blameless remembrance!
The only man with whom always all
Husbands behaved and women were virtuous."

Jovan Dučić

Aleksa ŠANTIĆ   1868 / 1924

Ostajte ovdje!

Ostajte ovdje!...Sunce tudjeg neba
Neće vas grijat k'o što ovo grije;
Grki su tamo zalogaji hljeba
Gdje svoga nema i gdje brata nije.

Od svoje majke, ko će naci bolju?!
A majka vaša zemlja vam je ova;
Bacite pogled po kršu i polju,
Svuda su groblja vaših pradjedova.

Za ovu zemlju oni bjehu divi,
Uzori sv'jetli, što branit je znaše,
U ovoj zemlji ostanite i vi,
I za nju dajte vrelo krvi vaše.

K'o pusta grana, kad jesenja krila
Trgnu joj lisje i pokose ledom,
Bez vas bi majka domovina bila;
A majka plače za svojijem čedom.

Ne dajte suzi da joj s oka leti;
Vrat'te se njojzi u naručja sveta;
Živite zato da možete mr'jeti
Na njenom polju gdje vas slava sreta!

Stay here!

Stay, oh stay here!...The sun of alien skies
Will never warm you as our sun does;
Bitter shall be each bite of your bread there,
Where you're alone and there is no brother.

Than one's own mother, who can find better?
And to you this country is your own mother;
Throw a glance at each field and barren rock,
Everywhere are graves of your forefathers.

Giants they were for this country of yours,
Heroic examples who knew how to defend her,
In this, your own country, you must also stay,
And, for her, shed the last drop of your blood.

As a bare branch when the wings of autumn
Tear away the leaves and strip her with ice,
Such would your mother be without you;
And a mother cries for a child who is gone.

Do not let tears flow from her eyes;
Go back to her, come to her sacred arms;
Live so that one day you may die for her,
On her fields where glory awaits you!

Ovdje vas svako poznaje i voli,
A tamo niko poznati vas neće;
Bolji su svoji i krševi goli
No cv'jetna polja kud se tudjin kreće.

Ovdje vam svako bratski ruku steže—
U tudjem sv'jetu za vas pelen cvjeta;
Za ove krše sve vas, sve vas veže:
Ime i jezik, bratstvo i krv sveta.

Ostajte ovdje!...Sunce tudjeg neba
Neće vas grijat k'o što ovo grije,—
Grki su tamo zalogaji hljeba
Gdje svoga nema i gdje brata nije...

Aleksa Šantić

Here you are known and by everyone loved,
And there you will be recognized by none;
Better are one's own dry and barren rocks
Than blossoming meadows where strangers tread.

Here everyone grasps your hand like a brother—
In foreign lands only wormwood blooms;
Everything you are binds you to these rocks;
Name and tongue, kinship and sanctity of blood.

Stay, oh stay here!...The sun of alien skies
Will never warm you as our sun does,—
Bitter shall be there, each bite of your bread
Where you're alone and there is no brother...

Aleksa Šantić

Veče na Školju

Pučina plava
Spava
   Prohladni pada mrak.
Vrh hridi crne
Trne
   Zadnji rumeni zrak.

I jeca zvono
Bono,
   Po kršu dršće zvuk;
S uzadhom tuge
Duge
   Moli ubogi puk.

Kleče mršave
Glave
   Pred likom Boga svog—
Ištu. Al' tamo,
Samo
   Ćuti raspeti Bog.

I san sve bliže
Stiže,
   Prohladni pada mrak.
Vrh hridi crne
Trne
   Zadnji rumeni zrak.

Aleksa Šantić

An Evening at Školje

Blue open seas
Sleep,
   Cool falls the twilight.
Over black cliffs
Die
   The last red rays.

And the bells sob,
Moan,
   Their toll quivers on rocks;
In deep sorrow
Sighing
   Prays the humble crowd.

Kneeling, bending meager
Heads,
   They face their God—
They yearn. But there
Silent
   Remains their crucified God.

And slumber comes slowly,
Descends,
   The chilly twilight falls.
Over black cliffs
Die
   The last red rays.

Aleksa Šantić

Ne vjeruj...

Ne vjeruj u moje stihove i rime
Kad ti kažu, draga, da te silno volim,
U trenutku svakom da se za te molim
I da ti u stabla urezujem ime—

Ne vjeruj! No kasno, kad se mjesec javi,
I prelije srmom vrh modrijeh krša;
Tamo gdje u grmu proljeće leprša,
I gdje slatko spava naš jorgovan plavi,

Dodji, čekaću te! U časima tijem,
Kad na grudi moje priljubiš se čvršće,
Osjetiš li, draga, da mi t'jelo dršće,
I da silno gorim ognjevima svijem;

Tada vjeruj meni, i ne pitaj više!
Jer istinska ljubav za riječi ne zna;
Ona samo plamti, silna, neoprezna,
Niti mari, draga, da stihove piše!

Aleksa Šantić

Do Not Believe...

Do not believe in my verses and rhymes
When they tell you, darling, how deeply I love you,
That at every moment I pray God for you
And that I carve your name in the trunks of trees—

Do not believe! But late at night, when the moon shines,
And pours silver over blue rocky mountains;
There, where in the shrubs a new spring flutters,
And where our blue lilacs are sweetly asleep,

Come, I'll wait for you! And in these hours,
When against my chest you press yourself tightly,
If you feel then, love, that my body trembles,
And burns with passion in the grasp of its fire;

Then, believe me, love, that's all you need to know!
For real love knows not how to use words;
It only burns like a blaze, not cautious,
Nor does it care, love, for verse and rhyme.

Aleksa Šantić

Proljeće

Nemoj, draga, noćas da te san obrva,
I da sklopiš oči na dušeku mekom!
Kada mjesec sine nad našom rijekom,
I na zemlju pane tiha rosa prva,

Rodiće se mlado proljeće! I svuda
Prosuće se miris plavih jorgovana;
I pahulje sn'ježne padaće sa grana
U naš bistri potok što baštom krivuda.

Uzviće se Ljeljo nad našim Mostarom,
I svaki će prozor zasuti beharom,
Da probudi srca što ljube i gore...

Zato nemoj, draga, da te san obrva!
Dodji, i u bašti budi ruža prva,
I na mome srcu miriši do zore!

Aleksa Šantić

Spring

My love, let not sleep overpower you tonight,
Nor close your eyes on your silk cushions!
When the moon starts shining above our river,
And early dew falls over our ground,

Young, the spring will arise! And everywhere
The scent will pour from blue lilac blooms;
Fragile snowflakes will keep falling from boughs
Into the clear brook that wanders through the garden.

The Lelo will soar above our Mostar,
Each window pane covered with flowering petals,
To awaken hearts that are in love and aflame...

That's why, love, let not sleep overpower you!
Come to me and be the first rose in the garden
And on my heart breathe your scent till dawn arrives.

Aleksa Šantić

Gospodjici

Nekada sam i vas na koljenu cupk'o,
I donosio vam slatke šećerleme,
I ljubio dugo vaše plavo tjeme,
I čelo, i lice nevino i ljupko.

No dani su prošli k'o rijeka nagla,
K'o trenutni snovi, kao puste varke:
Sad na vašem licu sjaj mladosti žarke,
A na mome jesen i turobna magla.

Ja znam, vaše srce sada vatrom gori,
Moje hladna zima okiva i mori;
Vaše oči sjaju k'o dva neba plava,

A moje su mutne kao magle sinje;
Mladost—ljubav—oganj—sve u grobu spava.
Po kosama mojim popanulo inje...

Aleksa Šantić

For a Young Lady...

There was a time when I rocked you on my knee,
And used to bring you sweet tasting candy,
Kissed for a long time the top of your blond head,
Your brow, and your face, so innocent and charming.

But days rushed by like a heedless torrent,
Like instantaneous dreams, like futile illusions:
Now your face beams with radiant youth
And on mine, reign autumn and gloomy fog.

I know, at present, your heart is ablaze,
Mine is shackled and benumbed by winter;
Your eyes are now like two sparkling, blue skies,

While mine are opaque and as grey as fog;
Youth—love—fire—all sleep in a grave.
All over my hair fell a white hoarfrost...

Aleksa Šantić

Jesen

Prošla je bura, stišale se strasti,
I ljubav s njima sve je bliže kraju;
Drukčije sada tvoje oči sjaju—
U njima nema ni sile ni vlasti.

Ja čujem: naša srca biju tiše,
Tvoj stisak ruke nije onaj prvi;
Hladan, bez duše, bez vatre i krvi,
K'o da mi zbori: nema ljeta više!

Za društvo nekad ne beše nam stalo,
O sebi samo govorasmo dugo;
No danas, draga, sve je, sve je drugo:
Sada smo mudri i zborimo malo.

...Prošlo je ljeto! Mutna jesen vlada.
U srcu našem ni jednog slavulja.
Tu hladan vjetar svele ruže ljulja,
I mrtvo lišće po humkama pada...

Aleksa Šantić

Fall

The storm is over, passions have subsided,
With them love is coming closer to an end;
Your eyes shine now in a different way—
They lost the force and the power they had.

I hear: our hearts beat now with lesser strength,
The touch of your hand is not what it was;
Cold, with no soul, no fire or blood,
Trying to tell me: the summer is over!

Once we were indifferent to company,
We only spoke at length about us;
Now, my love, all, all is changed:
Now we are wise and speak but little.

...Summer is over! A foggy fall reigns.
Not one nightingale is left in our hearts,
But cold winds which sway wilted roses
And dead leaves that fall on burial mounds...

Aleksa Šantić

Vojislav ILIĆ Mladji   1877 / 1944

Iz jedne šetnje

Gore sjaj sunca, čar zelenog krša,
Dole iz krila sumorne divljine
Otrgnut Timok bruji, i iskače
Iz crne, hladne, memljive pećine.

"Hajd'mo"—ja rekoh —"Timokovom vrelu!
Eno okomka kraj obale ove!
Tu ćemo sesti okruženi vodom
Slušati žubor i sanjati snove!"

"Ne,"—reče ona—"strašim se tog vrela!
K'o grobni zadah da iz njega piri!
No hajd'mo gore, gde je svetlost sunca
Gde lete orli, vetar i leptiri!"

"Al', draga,"—ja rekoh—"put je tamo strmen...
I dok ja nisam u selu još bio,
Da l' te je, reci, moj suparnik srećni
Putanjom onom gore izvodio?"

"Ah, ludo moja"—začuh prekor nežni—
"Tom večnom sumnjom što žalostiš mene?
Da, put je strmen, al' hajde, da vidiš
Da ne premaša snagu jedne žene!"

From a Walk

Above us radiant sun, the charm of green encrusted rocks.
From below, from the breast of the dismal wilderness
The Timok, torn away, rumbles and springs
From a blackened, cold, and molding cave.

"Let us go"—I said—"to the source of the Timok!
You see, there is a bank along this shore!
There we can sit, encircled by water,
And listen to it murmur and dream its dreams!"

"No,"—she said—"I fear this source!
It seems that grave's breath flows from it!
Better to climb upward and into the sunlight
Where the wind, the eagles, and the butterflies fly!"

"But, my dear,"—I said—"the path is steep...
Tell me, before I came to this village
Was it one of my happy rivals
Who led you along this path?"

"Ah, fool"—I heard her tender reproach—
"Why do you depress me with this eternal doubt?
Yes, the path is steep, but come and see,
It is not beyond the strength of a woman!"

I tada stište s kamena na kamen,
U hitrom skoku—k'o laka gazela,
Oči joj sjahu. Jedan blistav pramen
Beše joj prosut preko lepog čela.

Pred njom se uz put spletahu stostruko
Vinjaga, pavit, i bujad zelena;
Kupina trnjem zadiraše grubo
U njene skute tanušne k'o pena.

Zalud je vraćah! Gvozdeno uporstvo
Sjaše iz njenog zažarenog oka;
Dok na po puta, jogunica lepa,
Susta i klonu...i dalje ni kroka.

Vetar se titr'o haljinicom njenom,
I zlatnom kosom mekanom k'o svila;
Sunce se baš tada spustilo za brda,
I sva se šuma ućutala bila.

"Dosta! Ne treba!"—ja rekoh; a srce
Tad mi je bilo, da prsa raskine!
Jedan je slavuj baš tad priželjkiv'o
U tome času večernje tišine;

A Timok je jec'o, teško zaogrnut
Mrakom, k'o adskom zlokobnom haljinom...
"Nad čim uzdišeš?" upita me ona.
"Nad svojom srećom, i tvojom vrlinom!"

Vojislav Ilić Mladji

And she began to jump from stone to stone
In quick leaps—as light as a doe,
Her eyes were bright. A shimmering strand of hair
Swept across her lovely brow.

Before her a maze of stems were intertwined
Vines, traveler's joy, and dense greenery;
The thorns of the blackberries cut roughly into
Her skirt which was light as foam.

In vain I called her back! Iron stubbornness
Shone from her blazing eyes;
Then, halfway, the self-willed beauty
Grew weary and collapsed...not a step farther.

The wind played with her light dress
And with her soft, golden hair of silk;
Just then, the sun paused behind the mountains,
And the entire forest grew silent.

"Enough! It is not necessary!"—I said,
And my heart tore within my breast!
Then a nightingale sighed
In a moment of complete evening silence.

And the Timok wept, heavily enshrouded
In a darkness like the black veil of Hades...
"Why do you sigh?" she asked.
"After my happiness and your virtue!"

Vojislav Ilić Junior

Noćna svirka

Kad lepa "Gospa", u ponoćno doba,
Sa puno čežnje zavesu otškrine,
Do nje tad dopru zanošljivi zvuci
S "Gospodinove" violine.

A u toj svirci drkte bol i čežnja,
Zanos pun strasti i ljubavi seta;
Kao da kaže: "Ta zar nismo mladi?
Pustimo ljubav slobodno nek' cveta.

"Koleginice! Ljupka, mlada ženo!
Zašto kopniš tako u odaji sama?
Izidji da vidiš draž aprilske noći!
Zar ti nije teška samoća i tama?

"Prozori su moji otvoreni vazda.
Unutra postelja ugodna i meka.
Ruka mi nemarno prevlači vrh žica—
Al' srce...srce...ono na Vas čeka!

"Ta zaboravite prošlost, dužnost, muža!
Dodjite amo, lepa mlada ženo!
I u mojim grud'ma žar mladjani tinja,
I moje je srce čežnjom opijeno.

Night Music

In the middle of the night when the beautiful "Lady,"
Filled with longing parts her drapes slightly,
Beguiling sounds reach out to her
From the "Gentleman's" fragile violin.

In the music, trembling with anguish and longing,
Is the ardor and passion of love's remembrance,
As if intimating, "Are we not young?
Let us release our love to blossom unrestrained.

"Charming young woman! My colleague!
Why do you languish alone in your room?
Come and view the charms of an April night!
Do you not feel the burden of the night, loneliness?

"For you my window remains open always;
Inside a bed comfortable and soft.
My fingers play upon these strings thoughtlessly—
But my heart...my heart...awaits you.

"Forget the past, your obligations, your husband!
Come here lovely young woman!
Embers of youth burn in my breast as well,
My heart, too, is intoxicated with desire.

"Il' mislite, možda, ja sam hladna stena,
Da krv ne teče u žilama mojim;
Ne varajte se! Sit sam selskih cura!
Ja bih da Vašu naklonost prisvojim!

"Dodjite amo, lepa mlada ženo,
Da srknete ljubav sred noćnoga mira!
Ne bojte se ništa! Jer ima daleko
Od Vašega muža do Krivoga Vira!"

I prestadoše zvuci violine,
Kao da čekaju šta će biti sada...
A na prozoru nerešljivo stoji,
Stoji i misli učiteljka mlada.

Da li da ide? A prošlost? A vernost?
. . . .
Zar da zaboravi na onog čoveka
. . . .

Koji je na njenim devojačkim grud'ma
Sanjao nebo, Boga, rajske dveri;
I čiju ljubav čistu i duboku
Sva večnost ne bi mogla da premeri.

Zar *sve* da zgazi?...I ona se misli...
Slatka je neka jeza poduhvata;
Misli -i šapnu: "Oprosti mi, Bože!"
Pogleda u noć, i otškrinu vrata.

Or perhaps you think I am as cold as stone,
That blood fails to course through my veins;
Do not be misled! I am tired of village girls!
And only your favor is my one desire!

Come here lovely young woman,
And taste love amid the hush of night!
Do not be fearful! It is a long way
From your husband to the *Krivi Vir!*"

And then the sounds of the violin ceased
As if pausing to await what will happen next...
And at her window, hesitating,
Steeped in thoughts, stood the lovely young teacher.

Should she go? But what of the past? And faithfulness?
. . . .
Could she forget the other man
. . . .

The man who upon her maiden breast
Dreamed of the sky, God, the gates of Heaven;
Whose love was so pure and so deep
That it surpassed eternal understanding.

Trample such memories underfoot?...she wondered...
A sweet shiver ran down her body;
She thought again and whispered, "God forgive me!"
And opening the door, she gazed into the night.

I k'o kad ptica, plašljiva i laka,
Raširi krilca u noćnoj tišini,
I ona prhnu i iščeznu nekud,
Preko sokaka -k svojoj "Violini."

I snažna ruka seoskoga uče
Pojavi se na mah u trenutku tome,
Pridrža pticu, i prozor polako,
Nečujno-tiho, zatvori za njome.

I ptice nesta...ptice moje mile!
-Da l' ima Boga i sred noćne tmine?
Tišina...Samo iz izbe dopire
Prigušen, sanjiv drhtaj violine,

Kao kad žica o žicu se tare...
-Al' ćuti, pesmo, dalje ne govori!
Nebo i zemlja spe u tome casu!
Samo brz Timok šumi i žubori...

Vojislav Ilić Mladji

Just as a light and tremulous thrush,
Spreads its tiny wings in the silence of the night,
She, too, fluttered away and beyond view,
Beyond the village street...to her "Violin."

And the strong arm of the village teacher
Appeared then, magically,
To support the thrush. And the window slowly
Soundlessly...silently, closed after her.

The thrush had vanished...my beloved thrush!
-Is there no God in the middle of the night?
Only silence...and from the bower,
The muted, illusory quiver of a violin,

As if one string brushed against another...
-But keep silent, poetry, confide nothing more!
The sky and the earth both sleep at once!
Only the rapid Timok's waters hum and gurgle...

Vojislav Ilić Junior

Zvoni

Žureći stazom iz kobnoga sela,
Kroz tužna polja kao zlato žuta,
Ja i moj čuvar, lic nevesela,
Umorni, najzad, sedosmo kraj puta.

Tu, čekajući na dolazak kola,
U suhoj travi ćutasmo nas dvoje:
On—žilav, snažan; ja—slab i pun bola.
Svaki u misli utonuo svoje.

Ni otkud glaska. Na žitne poljane
Omara julska žestnom pripekla;
A krv iz moje još skorăsnje rane,
Kaplja za kapljom, lagano je tekla.

Sumnje i molbe, gnjev, nemirnu radost—
Sve sam sad gled'o u tami za sobom;
I jednu bujnu, verolomnu mladost,
Početu pesmom, završenu grobom!

Pa sanjah: "Gde si, lepo doba sretno,
Kad smo, u smehu, i detinjskoj šali,
Išli duž reke, i kroz polje cvetno
Crvene bulke šančevima brali?

Bells Toll

Hurrying along the path from the fateful village,
Through morose fields, yellowed as pure gold,
My guard and I, our expressions sad,
Grew tired finally and sat beside the road.

There, awaiting the arrival of the coach,
We were silent amid the dead grass.
He—strong, hardened; I—weak and filled with torment,
Each immersed in a private daydream.

Pervading stillness. Upon wheatfields
July heat burns with oppressive intensity
As blood from my recent wound
Trickles slowly, drop by drop.

Doubt and prayers, anger, restless joys—
The remains I regarded of a dismal past
And a vibrant and unfaithful youth
Which began in song and ended in the grave!

And I wondered: "Where are you, beautiful, happy times
When we, who laughed and joked like children,
Walked along a stream in flower covered meadows
And picked red poppies which bloomed by ravines?

"Gde su sad dani i časovi mili
Kad bi, u šetnji, u šumicu zašli,
I jedno drugo toćož izgubili,
Pa bi se opet, uz klicanje, našli?

"Kad sam, sav zbunjen, s mukom od nje skriv'o,
Te da ne spazi da mi dršće ruka,
Dok bih joj uz put nevešto veziv'o
Smaknutu svilnu vrpcu oko struka?...

"Gde su trenuci kad se glasno divih
Blistavoj draži njenih sitnih zubi!
Kad svaki cvetak mirisaše: Živi!
A svaki slavuj cvrkutaše: Ljubi!

"Ljubavi! srećo, kojom život sladih!
Šumarci! staze obrasle u cveću!
Vi pratioci mojih dana mladih,
Nikad vas više ja imati neću!

"Ne, nema slatkih iluzija više,
Kad čovek znade da sred zemnog dola
Najveća sreća, i slasti najviše,
Postaju izvor najdubljega bola..."

...A sunce žeže...Spavaju doline,
Tegobne snove sva priroda snuje.
Samo, u času te mrtve tišine,
Dosadni cvrčak odnekud se čuje.

"Where are the days and the treasured moments
When, in our walks, we entered groves
And pretended we had lost one another,
Only with shouts of joy to find each other again?

"Days when with embarrassment, I could barely hide
From her the way my hand trembled
While, as we walked, I clumsily retied
The loose silk sash around her waist...

"Where are the moments when I admired aloud
The sparkle of her small teeth!
When each flower with its scent said: Live!
And each nightingale sang: Love!

"Love! The happiness which sweetened my life!
Tree groves! Paths overgrown with flowers!
You, the companions of my youthful days,
For me, you will never be back!

"No, there are no more sweet illusions
Once a man learns that, in this earthly vale,
The most intense happiness and the greatest delights
Become the source of the deepest pain..."

...The sun scorches...the valleys are asleep,
Heavy dreams are dreamt by the entire nature.
At the hour of this deathly silence,
From somewhere, a monotonous cricket was heard.

I gle! moj čuvar skide kapu s glave!
Kud ga to misli daleko odnose?
"Sta slušaš, brate?" upitah, pun strave.
A on mi reče: "Zvoni...Sad je nose..."

Ne pitah više! Samo sam uzda'n'o,
K'o da me strela kroz prsa probola!
Ležah k'o mrtav...A zatim, lagano,
S još dva čuvara, udjosmo u kola.

I tad k'o dusi juriti uzesmo,
Preko mostova, brda, i dolina,
U divljem trku...I pred veče besmo
Pod kršnim Rtnjem, slikom ispolina.

Pa napred!...Vozar ludo uzmahuje,
I bičem šiba, znojnu kljusad goni.
Stražari ćute...Ah, da l' se to čuje...
Kako odnekud zvoni...zvoni...zvoni?...

Vojislav Ilić Mladji

But then! My guard took the cap off his head!
Where do his thoughts lead him?
"What do you hear, brother?" I asked in fear.
And he replied: "The bells toll...now, they carry her away..."

I asked no more but merely sighed
As if an arrow pierced my breast!
I lay as if in death...and then slowly,
With two more guards we boarded the coach.

Then, like ghosts, we charged
Over bridges and hills, and through valleys
In a wild run...and at nightfall we reached
The foothills of the rocky Rtanj, an immense vista,

Then still farther! The driver gestured madly,
And flogged the racing, sweating nags with his whip.
The guards were silent...Ah! does one really hear...
Bells, from somewhere, tolling...tolling...tolling?

Vojislav Ilić Junior

Veljko PETROVIĆ   1884 / 1967

Na brodu

Petoro sedimo na krovu od broda,
Zgureni, sumorni, zlovoljni i mračni.
Zapljuskava, šumi, penuši se voda;
Kikoću oblaci, proletnji, prozračni.

Petoro sedimo: jedna seda dama,
Sa sledjenim bolom, k'o drevna Meduza,
I jedna devojka, s tananim usnama,
Upalih prsiju, i usahlih suza.

A kraj njih ćutećki blenusmo u ništa
Nas tri mlada starca uvelih obraza,
Kao ukinuti cvetovi s grobišta,
Umornih pogleda, tupih, bez izraza.

...Kad ukroči ona, gizdava i gorda,
U crvenu ruhu, sa crvenim štitom.
Titrao se vetrić po telu joj vitom,
Što se lelujaše k'o igra akorda.

U ružičnom senu kupala je lice,
I pustila da je žudno sunce ljubi;
A kroz žedne, sočne, i drske usnice
Uporni i beli blistali se zubi.

On a Ship

Five of us are sitting on the deck of a ship,
Slouched, gloomy, somber, in a dark mood.
Around us the waters splash, gurgle, and foam;
While the clouds gambol, translucent and vernal.

Five of us are there: a white-haired lady,
Frozen in her grief, like the ancient Medusa,
And next to her a girl with very thin lips,
Her chest sunken, tears, dry in her eyes.

Next to them, we stared silently into nothing,
We three young, old men with withered cheeks,
Resembling three flowers torn from a graveyard,
Our eyes tired, clouded, and void of expression.

...Then she stepped among us, elegant and haughty,
Wearing a red dress with a red parasol.
A breeze trembled over her slender body,
Which swayed rhythmically like music chords.

She bathed her face in the pink and rosy shade,
And allowed the sensuous sun to kiss her,
While between her thirsty, luscious, juicy lips,
Peered insistently the whiteness of her teeth.

U svoj svojoj pompi, k'o carica neka,
Svesna svoje moći, ponosna i hola,
K'o dočaran sanak vremena daleka,
Stala je po sredi našeg tmurnog kola.

I k'o da nam žića sva gorčina nesta,
Utrnuše stare i goruće zlosti,
I mi uzbudjeno prignusmo se s mesta.
Blagujuć' u njenoj raskošnoj mladosti.

A kad ona ode, mi još dugo potom
Gledasmo za njome sa krova od broda;
Zaslepljeni njenom zanosnom lepotom,
I muzikom strasnom njenog gipkog hoda.

...Ali pljuska dalje, penuši se voda,
Kikoću oblaci, proletnji, prozračni,
A mi ostadosmo na krovu od broda,
I opet zgureni, zlovoljni, i mračni.

Veljko Petrović

In all her pomp, resembling an empress,
Quite conscious of her power, proud and haughty,
She conjured a dream of long bygone times
As she stood in the center of our gloomy group.

As if all bitterness disappeared from our lives,
Suddenly old and smarting malice was spent,
And stirred, we all leaned toward her,
To revel in the beauty of her luxuriant youth.

When she left, and for a long time afterward,
Our eyes followed her from the deck of the ship;
As if blinded by her bewitching beauty,
And the passionate music of her supple steps.

...And once again the water splashed, gurgled and foamed,
And the clouds gamboled, translucent and vernal,
And we were left on the deck of the ship,
Once more slouched, gloomy, somber, in dark mood.

Veljko Petrović

O zašto?

O zašto smo se, zašto smo se sreli
Na mrtvoj stazi opora venjenja,
Pod mutnim nebom maćijskog jesenja!
O, zašto smo se pogledali, je li?

O, zašt' se nismo mimoišli, draga,
K'o dve ladje na sred okeana,
Što crnih jedri, a s dva mrtva kana,
Plove i minu u magli bez traga?

Veljko Petrović

Oh, Why?

Oh, why did we meet, why did we have to meet,
On the deathly path of sad decaying,
Under ailing skies of autumnal slaying!
Oh, why did we look and then, each other greet?

Oh, why did we not glide by each other, dear,
Like two ships on high seas, black sails at full span;
Ships that carry the bodies of two famous khans,
And then sink into the fog without a trace?

Veljko Petrović

Miloš PEROVIĆ   1874 / 1918

Našto misao...

Našto misao, kad nije duboka
  Kao večnost što je!
Našto, kad nije oštra kao koplje,
  Ni jasna k'o sunce,
Da njome prodrem u znamenje svoje!

Našto, kad je na jade nam data!
  Mati večnog straha;—
Kad ne dopire od pokrova dalje!
  Do groba mračna,
A tajna preko ništavoga praha.

Našto ta mudrost Božjeg Providjenja
  Crv kome se klanja!
Našto me vara sa prizrakom umlja?
  Našto mi oči
Kad večno tonem u tami neznanja!

Miloš Perović

What is the Purpose of Thought...

What is the purpose of thought unless it is deep
  As deep as eternity!
Unless it is as piercing as a spear,
  As sharp as a ray of sun,
With which to penetrate the meaning of my fate!

What is its purpose if it only gives pain!
  Begetter of eternal fear;—
When it cannot reach beyond the shroud!
  Opaque to the point of the grave,
And mystery when dust returns to dust.

Wherefore this wisdom of Divine Providence
  That worm to which we bow!
Why does it deceive with a semblance of reason?
  Why have I eyes
When eternally I sink in unknowing darkness!

Miloš Perović

Stevan LUKOVIĆ   1877 / 1902

Jesenja kišna pesma

Tužno...Jednolik, dug i vlažan
  Jesenji dan se tmuri;
Plače, bez kraja, bolno plače
  Sumoran beskraj suri;
U mrtvi suton što se hvata
  Jednači, jeca vesma
-Po trulom lišću, preko blata—
  Stara, bolna, i polagana,
Ubogih, mutnih, šturih dana
  Jesenja kišna pesma...

Spomeni davni tište, tište,
  I s njima vek se čami.
...Jeca i plače davnih dana
  Pospana, bolna, i lagana,
Jeca i plače u toj tami,
K'o gluhi žubor suza sami'
  Daleke sreće pesma...

Oh, jadno drago!...Večno tako,
  Kaj se, i kaj, i žali!
I dok za senim' nada pali'
  Pogrebna bruji pesma,
Spomene blede sreće hrani,
Poslednje svoje varke brani,
  I veni, veni vesma!...

The Autumnal Rain Song

Morose...Somber, damp and stale
  Sulks the autumnal day;
Cries, endlessly, painfully cries
  Eternity from leaden skies.
Ambivalent and slow the twilight fails
  To live, and morbidly wails
Over mud and dead leaves—
  Rings and brings back empty eves,
Days void and endlessly long
  The autumnal rain song...

Memories and dull, dull pain,
  An entire life to squander in vain
...With it a song of past days sobs
  Sleepy, anguishing and slow;
It throbs in this obscure glow
As soundless tears unseen
  This song of what has been...

Oh, forlorn love!...Eternally so,
Repent, repent, and regret!
While dying hopes we follow
  With funeral hymns which sound so hollow
We bury pale joys we hardly recall,
We fight for illusions which had to fall
  And wilt, wilt, wilt even more!...

Tužno...Jednolik, dug, i vlažan
  Jesenji dan se tmuri;
Plače bez kraja, bolno plače
  Sumorni beskraj suri;
I tužan, tužan ropac tajni
  Dalekih slušam dana;
Ugušen jeca šum beskrajni,
  Tiši i tiši vesma—
K'o stara, bolna, polagana,
Ubogih, mutnih, šturih dana
  Jesenja kišna pesma.

Stevan Luković

Morose...Somber, damp and stale
   Sulks the autumnal day;
Cries, endlessly, painfully cries
   Eternity from leaden skies.
The death rattle secretly perceived
   Of bygone days I hear,
Hushed sobs which sound so near
   But less and less believed—
It rings and brings back empty eves,
Days void and endlessly long
   The autumnal rain song.

Stevan Luković

Svetislav STEFANOVIĆ 1874 / 1944

Muzičke vizije
(1-2)
2

Jecaju i struje mesečevi zraci;
K'o srebrna harfa mesečina svira;
Plivaju i tonu magleni oblaci,
K'o akordi puni kroz carstvo etira.

Trepte tihe vode, i s čežnjom dubina
Upijaju u se zvukove što žedne,
Dršćući k'o krune vodenoga krina,
Pod dojmom blaženstva misterije jedne.

Rasklaplju se u snu očarane školjke;
Izdiše površjem, k'o od zlata pena—
I s nemoći tihom jedne slatke boljke
—Drkće mesečina zvucima Šopena.

Svetislav Stefanović

Musical Visions
(1-2)
2

Sobbing and flowing the moonlight beams;
As a silver lyre rings its languid gleam;
Float and slowly sink the wisps of foggy clouds,
As full ringing chords in the realm of sounds.

Calm waters quiver and shimmer and drink into
Their depths longing and thirsty sounds,
Tremble like dying water lily crowns,
Oppressed by delights of a mystery so strange.

In their secret dreams mysterious shells part;
On the surface dies a pale golden foam—
With the languid weakness of a longing heart
—Like Chopin's sad chords under a moonlit dome.

Svetislav Stefanović

Trijumf Venere
"U ime Večnoga..."

Dodji, o dodji! U presltakoj noći,
Sakriven tamom od tvoga pogleda,
Govoriću ti o večitoj moći
Života, i o sreći zemnih čeda,

Što mogu smrt da plodnošću pobede.
Govoriću ti, kako nema slasti
Većih od slasti stvaranja — i sve bede
Ne mogu da je smanje. Pa ću kaz'ti

Kako je duh božanstven u toj snazi,
I da mu telo tek dostojno služi,
Plodno i samo, -jer njegovi trazi
Duhu su vrelo...Zatim: kako kruži

Kroz vasionu celu isto biće,
I kako sve se u nj stapa i sliva,
I svi poznamo njegovo otkriće
U času kad od dvoga jedno biva.

I reč'ma punim tajnog, nejasnoga,
I nesvesnoga -svest ću ti zaneti.
Pa ti, sakriven od pogleda tvoga,
U ime Večnog nevinost uzeti.

Svetislav Stefanović

The Triumph of Venus
"In the name of the Eternal..."

Come, oh come! In this sweetest of all nights,
Hidden by darkness from the look in your eyes,
I shall speak to you of the eternal power
Of life and the bliss of the heirs to the earth,

Who can overcome death by procreation.
I shall tell you there is no delight
Greater than the delight of creating—no misery
Can diminish it. And then I shall say

How divine is the spirit in the mastery of such power,
And the body only a worthy servant,
Itself fertile since all viscera
Are the source of spirit...Then: how encompassing

The whole universe is one and the same being,
And how everything blends and unites within,
And how we are all aware of this revelation
At the moment when the two become one.

And with words that are secretive, vacuous,
And unconscious, I shall ravish your mind.
Then, hidden from the look in your eyes,
In the name of the Eternal, rob you of your purity.

Svetislav Stefanović

Milan ĆURČIN   1880 / 1960

Pustite me kako ja hoću!

Zašto uvek jedno i isto,
Zar sve baš mora biti jasno i čisto,
I svuda propisan broj!?
Ta pesma nije akt, i mis'o nije slovo.
I duh traži uvek novo,
I hoće da bude svoj.

Ritam će kroz muziku reči
Probiti sebi pute,
I otići u pravi kraj;
U pesmi zakoni ćute—
Pustite osećaj!

Milan Ćurčin

Let Me Do It My Way!

Why should one always repeat the same,
And everything be clear and tame,
With always the proper number and name?
A poem is not red tape, nor a thought a letter.
My soul wants something new and better,
The spirit wants to be free.

Rhythm through the music of words
Will find its own way,
And have its final say;
A poem is supposed to be—
Feeling set free.

Milan Ćurčin

"Pučina je stoka jedna grdna"

Ja demokrat nisam nigda bio,
Ma da sam nekad i sam drž'o da sam;
Ali tek danas smem priznati šta sam,
I reći što sam i od sebe krio:

Ja strepim od tog divljačnoga puka,
I s osećajem večnim, iste vrste
Što ima dete kad ukoči prste,
Pa pruža ruke plašeć' se bauka,
Ja žudim samo da me ne dodirne.

Ah, da mi nije mlade snage ove,
Što mrzi mlaki nerad duše mirne,
Sve bih mu dao, da ne bunim snove.

Mi nismo isto. Ni srce ni glava;
Moje su misli nestalne i nove;
Ja imam snova, a puk mirno spava.

Milan Ćurčin

The Mob is an Awful Bunch of Cattle

A democrat I have never been,
Although at times I thought I was;
But only today I dare confess what I am
And tell what I hid even from my own self:

I am afraid of that savage mob.
And with the feeling, eternally the same,
That a child has when it stiffens its fingers
And stretches its arms in fear of a ghostly form,
I long that it does not touch me.

Ah, had I not this youthful vigor
Which hates the tepid idleness of a quiet soul,
I would give anything that it does not disturb my dreams.

We are not one and the same in heart nor in mind;
My thoughts are always changing and new;
I have dreams while the mob sleeps in peace.

Milan Ćurčin

Milutin BOJIĆ 1892 / 1917

Vrane

Gledao sam dugo kako lete vrane,
Crne kao mladost kad u nevrat tone.
U daljini zapad katkad bleskom plane,
A nad njime sivi oblaci se gone.
   Bez krika, bez cilja letele su vrane.

Crne, istovetne, strašnu priču zbore,
Kako je užasno s drugim jednak biti.
Tišina: prolaznost i večnost se bore.
Sve kraj mene pada u njihove niti.
   Ala je užasno s drugim jednak biti!

Krik jedan, pun strasti, začu se u noći.
To vran jedan kriknu. Jato za njim grnu.
A on je kliktao, svestan svoje moći,
I vodio cilju braću svoju crnu.
   Ćuteći su vrane letele u noći.

Ja sam zadrhtao. Čini mi se tada
Da sam bio sličan kakvoj čednoj ženi,
Što, pošavši stazom na kojoj se pada,
Trza se, a stid joj obraze crveni.
   Te večeri Volja rodi se u meni.

Milutin Bojić

The Crows

For a long time I watched the crows flying,
Black as youth falling into an abyss.
Far away the west flared at moments,
Under grey clouds hunted by the wind.
    Without sound or aim the crows flew.

Black, all equal, they told the tragic story,
How terrifying it is to resemble the others.
Silence: mortals and eternity struggle.
The world around me falls into their net.
    How terrifying it is to resemble the others!

A cry, bursting with passion, tore the night.
The voice of a crow. The flock rushed after him.
And he cried, conscious of his powers,
And led his black brothers to their goal.
    Soundlessly the crows flew through the night.

I shivered. I felt at that moment
I resembled an unknown, chaste woman
Who, stepping on the path that leads to her downfall,
Shudders, while shame flushes her face.
    That night my Will was born in me.

Milutin Bojić

Jesenje šetnje

1

Sve strasnije volim poznu jesen, što se,
Sva mokra i siva, kao avet grči
I zaledjen vidik sužava i mrči
I grešnike šiba, što milosti prose.

Volim divlje patke, što vrh voda kriče,
I pokisle vrane i magle močari,
O beskrajno volim te sumorne čari
Kad vidici sivi na grobnice liče.

I koračam gordo po nądama palim,
Razdragan što život oko mene trune,
Tamne oči sunca i proleća pune,
A ja ni što želim, niti za čim žalim.

2

Blista zadnje lišće kao zlatna mreža
Na jesenjoj zemlji i k'o da miriše
Na sunčanu jaru koje nema više
I cedi iz zemlje kap otrova sveža,

Autumnal Strolls

1

More and more I love late fall which,
All wet and grey and distorted as a ghost,
Shrinks and dims the frozen horizon
And whips the sinners who beg for mercy.

I love the call of wild ducks over waters,
And rain-soaked crows, the fog over swamps,
Oh, how infinitely I love these sad charms
When grey horizons look like somber tombs.

I stroll proud over fallen hopes,
Happy that life rots all around me,
My eyes dark but filled with sun and spring;
Then, I have neither desire nor regret.

2

The last leaves shimmer as a golden net
Over the ground and still smell
Of sunny haze that is so long gone;
They draw from earth a fresh drop of poison.

A ledena magla pobožno razume
Taj ponosni odmor posle strasnih dneva,
Zadnju raskoš snage koja dogoreva,
Tu poslednju pesmu stare, gorde šume—

I gustim joj velom obavija grane,
Tako ćutke trne, bez tudjega plača,
Jedna zrela pesma od jauka jača,
Mre, nikom ne rečen, bol na mlade dane.

Volim tu svečanost sutonske osame,
Kad osećam sebe, što u srcu spava;
Tad u meni tisuć tuga vaskrsava
I niz uspomena umire sred tame,

Kao miris žene koja iščezava.

Milutin Bojić

The freezing fog piously understands
This proud rest after passionate days,
This last blaze of a withering power,
The last song of my proud forest—

Dead branches are wrapped in a dense veil,
So in silence fades, without an alien tear,
This ripe song stronger than a sob,
So dies, untold, the lament of young days.

I do love this feast of twilight solitude,
When my heart is lonely and half asleep;
Then a thousand sorrows arise in me
And a string of memories dies in the dark,

Like the perfume of a woman slowly disappearing.

Milutin Bojić

Poljubac

Mi smo deca sreće i života zrela,
Naša čudna ljubav do niskosti naga,
Mrzi legendarnih noći čeda svela:
Za nju mladost Bog je, a strast joj je snaga.

...Januar fijuče u sutonskoj studi,
Bičevana reka modri se i peni.
Jauk golih grana mrtve iz sna budi:
Kikoće se vreme u večitoj smeni.

Sve tutnji u snazi napregnute volje,
Krši se i pišti i seva i para,
Razjaren se orkan s nebesima kolje,
Polusmrznut Neptun s Adom razgovara.

Opijeni mržnjom, opkoljeni vriskom,
Pripijene usne do krvi smo grizli,
Moćna su nam rebra drhtala pod stiskom
Prstiju, što medj njih neznano su sklizli.

Taj poljubac duše pio nam je do dna,
I hiljade šara, vrelih k'o strast lavlja,
Igrahu k'o oči dva pantera srodna,
Dok nebesa siva bivahu sve plavlja.

The Kiss

We were born to be happy, to love life fully,
Our love is bizarre, naked and coarse,
And we hate those born for frozen nights:
Youth is our god, and passion our strength.

...January storms howl through frozen eventide,
And whip the river into ice-blue froth,
While moaning trees arouse the dead:
Bitter is the laughter of vanishing time.

The world is a clash of conflicting wills,
Bellows and screams, thunders and death.
While rabid gales tear the skies apart,
Frozen tides duel with burning hell!

Intoxicated with hatred, surrounded by screams,
In a sensual kiss our bleeding lips are glued,
And strong ribs strain under the pressure
Of unconscious fingers that grip them with passion.

In that kiss we exchange our burning souls.
Myriads of embers and glowing cinders
Dance and flash as the eyes of tigers,
While grey skies are turning pale blue.

Plašljivih fauna, videh, jure čete
Upivši u mene sav svoj pogled zečji,
Pevajući psalme neke vere svete,
Koje gušio je njihov pogled dečji.

Vekovima tako kikoću se oni,
Splet njihov nevidljiv vaseljenom ide
I, tek kad u nama zvuk srca zazvoni,
Njihove se čete oživljene vide.

Mi smo deca sreće i života zrela,
Naša čudna ljubav do niskosti naga,
Mrzi legendarnih noći čeda svela;
Za nju mladost Bog je, a strast joj je snaga.

Milutin Bojić

Then I see flocks of scared fauns dashing,
Starting like rabbits with terrified eyes,
Chanting psalms of an unknown religion
Buried deep in their childlike gaze.

For centuries already they've snickered like that.
Unseen their rabble swarms the universe
For to see them we need our hearts to bleed
And echo their fear and thus bring them to life.

We were born to be happy, to love life fully,
Our love is bizarre, naked and coarse,
And we hate those born for frozen nights;
Youth is our god, and passion our strength.

Milutin Bojić

Bajka o ženi

Ljubičastom parom diše Zemlja sana,
Modri su čempresi sagli glave tužno,
Vrh mrtvoga mora krikne koja vrana,
U zlatnome bakru tone sunce južno.

Usijan se pesak beli i preliva,
Zadrev u nebesa red planina spava,
Na crvenom žalu slet ždralova sniva,
Roj mušica dršće iznad rečnih stava.

Vruć, zapahnut mirom i muzikom boja,
Sa dosadom Čovek svu tu raskoš motri,
Leži sirov, krvav, pun dlake i znoja,
I traži u suncu da svoj odgled smotri.

Zrelost jednog dana prazna mu je sena,
Nejasnih oblika jedno Novo čeka,
Skup raskoši, sunca, nestalno k'o pena.
—I odjednom on se strašću zacereka.

Sa jelovih gora slazila je Žena.

Milutin Bojić

The Legend of Woman

Sleepy Earth breathed its purple vapors,
Blue evergreens lowered their heads,
Over dead seas, crows were flying sadly,
The southern sun was melting in golden bronze.

The burning sand glared and shimmered,
Tearing the skies, tall mountains slept,
On the red beach, dreamed a flock of cranes,
Flies were dancing over the river.

Hot, drowsy, in the music of peace and colors,
Bored, Man watched this luxury,
He lay, bloody, a mess of hair and sweat,
And tried to see himself in the sunny rays.

The ripe hour of the day was empty,
Man waited for a New Form,
A thing lush, sunny, like sea foam.
Suddenly he laughed with throaty passion.

Down evergreen slopes came the Woman.

Milutin Bojić

Biographies of Serbian Poets

BOJIĆ, MILUTIN (1892-1917). Bojić began publishing poems while still in high school and continued to publish as a student of Philosophy at the University of Belgrade. His poems were published in *Venac, Nova Iskra, Delo, Savremenik,* and *Srpski Književni Glasnik.* At this time Bojić was also a regular contributor to *Dnevni List* and *Pijemont* which published his critiques and reviews of theater plays. Bojić published his first collection of poems (*Pesme,* 1914) on the eve of World War I. The literary critic, Jovan Skerlić, wrote his final review on these poems and welcomed Bojić as a promising talent. Bojić's first collection of poems was marked by an avid love of life and its sensual pleasures. His versification opened new possibilities in language by the introduction of carefully studied Serbian medieval and biblical patterns of language and rhymes. The patriotic poems for which Bojić is best known, were written during World War I. Due to the war, the first editions of Bojić's works were either destroyed by the enemy or in the great fire of Thessaloniki (*Pesme bola i ponosa,* 1917). Although he published during World War I, his work became known during the post-war years through the posthumous publications of his poems and theater dramas in verse. **PUBLICATIONS:** *Pesme* (Beograd: 1914); *Kain* (Niš: 1915); *Pesme bola i ponosa* (Thessaloniki: 1917); *Kraljeva jesen* (Sarajevo: 1918); *Soneti* (Beograd: 1922); *Pesme i drame* (Beograd: 1927).

ĆURČIN, MILAN (1880-1960). Born in Pančevo, Ćurčin was educated in Novi Sad, and graduated from the Department of German and Slavic studies in Vienna. He was appointed associate professor at the University of Belgrade in 1907, where he stayed until 1914. During World War I, Ćurčin was a member of the Yugoslav Committee (*Jugoslovenski Odbor*) in London. From 1920 to 1941, he edited and published the Literary Review *Nova Evropa* in Zagreb. He was a poet, journalist, and free lance-writer. Influenced by the German *Secessionistic School*, Ćurčin was one of the first poets to introduce free verse into the early twentieth-century Serbian poetry. Bogdan Popović included him in his *Anthology* as an example of the *Modern*. PUBLICATIONS: *Pesme* (Beograd: 1906); *Das Serbische Volkslied in der Deutchen Literatur* (Leipzig: 1905); *Nemačka romantika* (Beograd: 1906); *Gete i gospodja Štajn* (1908); *Fauriel i njegove preteče u Nemačkoj* (SKG., 1911); *Daudet i ilirstvo* (LMS., 1913); *Od stare umetnosti ka "secesiji"* (*Umetnički pregled*, SKG., II, 6, 1911).

DUČIĆ, JOVAN (1871-1943). Born in Trebinje, Herzegovina, Dučić attended schools in Mostar and Sarajevo, and received a degree in Elementary Education in Sombor. He taught in different small towns in Bosnia and Herzegovina. Dučić settled in Mostar where he started the literary review *Zora* with Aleksa Šantić and Svetozar Ćorović in 1896. In 1899, he received scholarships to Switzerland and France, which gave impetus to his future career. Dučić graduated from the Law School of the University of Paris in 1906, and began his career as a diplomat and a poet. He served in Sofia, Rome, Athens, and Madrid. He was appointed as a delegate to the League of Nations in Geneva, and then became Minister in Budapest, Rome and Madrid. In his poetic development, Dučić was first influenced by the works of Vojislav Ilić. Later, while in Paris, he was further influenced by Lamartine, Gautier, and Musset. The essential change in his poetry was brought about by his contact with the French *Parnassians* and *Symbolists*. He was chiefly influenced by the poetry of Albert Samain and Henri de Regnier. In Serbian poetry, Dučić is a rare example of a *l'art-pour-l'art* poet, amid an atmosphere of dedicated, patriotic poetry. Dučić's poetry is considered to be, along with that of Milan Rakić, the greatest achievement of Serbian poetry in the period between 1900 and 1914. His verse is fluid, evocative, and melodious in its tonality as opposed to Rakić's metallic sounds. "Woman" is the essential force in his poetry, with all the aspects of the mysterious and mythical attraction of what the Germans call *die ewige weibliche*. In Serbian poetry, Jovan Dučić remains a master of the evocative power of the musical tonalities of words and their secondary connotations. Dučić also published a number of letters from Geneva, the Alps, the Ionean Sea, Spain, Rome, Paris, Palestine, and Egypt. These letters reflect states of emotional subjectivity and are poetical evocations rather than travelogues. His prose work, *Blago cara Radovana*, is an individual concept of his philosophy of life. This work harkens back to the eighteenth-century books of aphorisms and maxims. **PUBLICATIONS:** *Pjesme* (Mostar: 1901); *Plave legende* (Beograd: 1908); *Pesme* (SKZ: Beograd: 1908); *Pesme*, (Beograd: 1911); *Sabrana Dela* (Beograd: 1929); *Carski soneti, Plave legende, Gradovi i himere* (Beograd: 1930); *Blago cara Radovana* (Beograd: 1932); *Pesme* (Pittsburgh: 1943); *Grof Sava Vladislavić-Raguzinski* (Pittsburgh: 1943).

ILIĆ, VOJISLAV (1860-1894). As the son of the neo-classical poet Jovan Ilić, Ilić grew up in the refined literary atmosphere of his father's home in Belgrade. His love and rendering of motifs of ancient Greek and Roman cultures came from the influence of his early surroundings. At a time when Serbian literature and poetry were subjective, patriotic, Romantic and exalted, Ilić declared himself to be in complete opposition to it with his "poetry of calm emotions" (*poezija mirnog čuvstva*). Ilić was the first modern Serbian poet who introduced new versification and new themes into the modern Serbian poetry at the turn of the century. He introduced an objective and depictive poetry, often akin to landscape paintings. The poetry of Ilić comprises four separate fields: patriotic poetry; political and satirical poetry; poetry with themes from Greek and Roman civilizations; and personal lyrical poetry. The latter motif also appears in the poetry of Rajić, Pandurović and other poets of pessimism of the following period. Traces of Romantic poetry are rarely found in the versification and thematics of Ilić's poetry. In this respect the break is complete. Originator of an entirely new movement called *Vojislavism*, Ilić influenced the subsequent Serbian poets of the turn of the century at one or another moment in their creativity, with the exception of Milan Rakić. **PUBLICATIONS:** *Pesme* (Beograd: 1889); *Pesme* (Beograd: 1892).

ILIĆ, VOJISLAV MLADJI (1877-1944). Ilić Mladji was educated in Belgrade where he graduated from Law School in 1903. For a time, he served in various provincial Courts of Law and, after World War I, was appointed Secretary to the Court of Appeals in Belgrade. From 1920 to 1944, he was Inspector of the Ministry of Justice in Belgrade. Ilić Mladji published his first works in the periodicals *Zvezda, Delo, Bosanska Vila,* and *Brankovo Kolo.* He also published translations of foreign literature, most of which are contained in his book *Tudjinski biser* (1901). As a poet, Ilić Mladji was prolific, but uneven in his choice of themes and style. He was under the influence of nineteenth-century Romanticism, although he located his lyrical motifs in a realistic milieu. His best poems deal with his personal tragic love experience. The three poems included in this *Anthology* represent the emotional experience of this love tragedy. **PUBLICATONS:** *Tudjinski biser* (Beograd: 1901); *Pesme* (Čačak: 1909); *Krvavi cvetovi* (Beograd: 1914); *Novi krvavi cvetovi* (Beograd: 1915); *Pesme* (Beograd: 1919); *Pripovetke* (Beograd: 1922); *Celokupna lirika* (Beograd: 1924); *Jesenski cvetovi* (Beograd: 1936).

JAKŠIĆ, DJURA (1832-1878). Jakšić was equally well-known as a painter and poet in his time, with a subsequent emphasis on his work in poetry. He studied painting in Budapest from 1847 through 1849 under the Italian master Jaccopo Marastoni. In 1850, he studied with Constantine Danil who infuenced his further work greatly. Jakšić continued his studies in painting in Vienna, where he was influenced by Karl Rahl. Unable to make a living as a painter, Jakšić began a career as an elementary school teacher in various small towns in Serbia, and finally moved to Belgrade in 1872, where he resided until his death. As a painter, Jakšić represented the Serbian Romantic painting school of the second half of the nineteenth century. As a poet, he belonged to the same Romantic school by his patriotic and exalted poems, among which are a few love poems. His poetic work was influenced by Jovan Jovanović-Zmaj, Petöffi, and Byron. Some of his poems (*Padajte braćo, Otadžbina*) remain unsurpassed in Serbian patriotic poetry. His work comprises a large collection of lyrical poems, six epic poems, thirty-two short stories, and three theater plays. **PUBLICATIONS:** *Seoba Srbalja* (Novi Sad: 1867); *Jelisaveta, knjeginja crnogorska* (Beograd: 1868); *Pripovetke* (Beograd: 1874); *Dela, I-IV* (Beograd: 1882-83).

LUKOVIĆ, STEVAN (1877-1902). Luković began publishing poetry in high school literary societies and later in the literary reviews *Delo*, *Zvezda*, and *Nova Iskra*. He published politically oriented poems in the *Social Demokrat* and *Radničke novine*. Among those was a well received translation of Victor Hugo's *Les Châtiments*. Luković soon became dissatisfied with his work and stopped publishing entirely. He graduated from the Law School of the University of Belgrade and was appointed clerk to the State Council. His health was poor and his political opinions in opposition to the Obrenović regime which barred any possible professional development for him. During this period, he published several articles in the opposition newspaper *Dnevni List*. Although the articles were published anonymously, he lost his position of clerk with the government. Luković secretly continued perfecting his poems. After his premature death at the age of twenty-five, his friends discovered his poems among his papers and published them in 1903. Jovan Skerlić, a close friend of Luković's, stated that he found: "...fluid verses, similar to those of Paul Verlaine; notes from Paul Bourget's *Essays on Modern Psychology*, and verses from Victor Hugo's *Feuilles d'Automne*". The success of this collection of poems was instantaneous. Luković introduced into Serbian poetry the melancholic fluidity of the French Instrumentalist School in form, and the pessimism and disenchantment with life in content. Both elements echo in the poetry of Svetislav Stefanović, Vladislav Petković-Dis, and other later poets at the turn of the century. **PUBLICATIONS:** *Pesme* (Beograd: 1903).

PEROVIĆ, MILOŠ (1874-1918), published also under the pseudonym of Pietro Kosorić. Perović studied in Belgrade, Vienna, Leipzig, and Zurich, where he obtained a Ph.D. degree with a thesis on Dositej Obradović in 1902. Employed as a teacher in Užice and Čačak (1902-1906), he was transfered to Skoplje in 1906, to Thessaloniki in 1908, and back to Skoplje that same year. Perović, a reserve officer in the Balkan Wars and World War I, was wounded and subsequently died in Paris in 1918. His poetry reflects concerns with the metaphysical reasons of life and death. He received the award of the Serbian Royal Academy of Sciences for his tragedy in verse *Karadjordje* in 1906. **PUBLICATIONS:** *Pesme* (Užice: 1903); *Die Pedagogischen Ansichten des Dositeus Obradović* (doctoral dissertation, Zurich: 1906); *Pesme II* (Beograd: 1909); *Karadjordje, tragedija u stihu* (Beograd: 1907); *Ženomrzac, pozorišna šala* (Skoplje: 1914); *Misli* (Beograd: 1934).

PETROVIĆ, VELJKO (1884-1967), studied at the Law School in Budapest and became a free-lance writer after 1907. Petrović often contributed to *Srbobran* in Zagreb and became the editor of *Sloboda*, the official organ of the Independent Serbian party in Sombor. In 1909, he joined the staff of the periodical *Srpska Riječ* in Sarajevo. In 1911, Petrović moved to Belgrade. During the war, he contributed to *Branik* and *Savremena pitanja*, but then followed the retreat of the Serbian army through Albania. For the rest of the war, he lived in Geneva where he was a member of the propaganda bureau of the *Yugoslav Committee (Jugoslovenski Odbor)* which he had joined in 1918. Between the two World Wars, Veljko Petrović was active in different fields of Yugoslav cultural life. During World War II, he spent time in the German concentration camp at Banjica. After World War II, he was appointed Director of the National Museum in Belgrade, a position he occupied until 1962. In his poetry, Petrović expressed his revolt against the banality of everyday life and its stagnation, yet his poetry is essentially patriotic in its demand for the liberation of regions inhabited by Serbs and under foreign domination until 1918. He published numerous articles and essays on writers, painters and sculptors and their works. **PUBLICATIONS:** *Rodoljubive pesme* (Beograd: 1912); *Na pragu, zbirka pesama* (Zemun, Beograd i Pančevo: 1913); *Sabrana Dela I-II* (Beograd: 1930); *Sabrana Dela III-IV* (Beograd: 1932); *Stihovi* (Beograd: 1951); *Rodoljubive pesme* (Novi Sad: 1952); *Nevidljivi izvor, zbirka pesama* (Novi Sad: 1956); *Dela I-II* (Novi Sad i Beograd: 1963).

RAJIĆ, VELIMIR (1879-1915). After graduating from high school, Rajić enrolled in the Philosophical Department of the Velika Škola in Belgrade, where he concentrated on studies of French language and literature. His first appointment after graduation was in a high school in Belgrade as a French teacher. Because of his worsening health, he was moved first to the Ministry of Education in 1906, and then for the same reason to the National Library in Belgrade. Rajić started publishing his first works in the literary periodicals *Lasta* and *Bosanska vila*, and continued publishing translations in Janko Veselinović's *Zvezda*. During the Balkan Wars of 1912-1913, he joined the army but was not sent to combat lines because of his health. During World War I, Rajić started editing *Ratne Zapise* just before his death. In 1908, Rajić published his *Pesme i proza* as a separate volume. It contains twenty-five poems and two novelettes; however, his other works remained disseminated throughout literary periodicals. These works comprise sixteen articles, reviews and short essays, as well as two dramas. His poetry is pessimistic, disenchanted with life, and relates to his personal unhappy love. **PUBLICATIONS:** a complete list of Rajić's publications is given in: *Venac*, 4-5 (1922-23) as *Bibliografija radova Velimira J. Rajića.*

RAKIĆ, MILAN (1876-1938). After studying philosophy, Rakić graduated from the Law School of the University of Paris in 1901. He began his career in the Export Bank in Belgrade in 1902; was appointed to the Ministry of Finance until 1904; and then joined the Foreign Office where he remained from 1904 to 1933. He served as consul in Macedonia; Minister in Copenhagen, Christiania, and Sofia; and Minister in Rome. His first poems were published in 1902 in *Srpski Književni Glasnik* under the pseudonym Z. Rakić had a deep knowledge of French poetry and was particularly under the influence of the French Parnassian School. There are some critics who see in his work the influence of French Symbolism. He is considered, with Dučić, as one of the two greatest poets of Serbian early twentieth-century poetry. His aesthetic concepts and his form are similar to the Parnassians. Following the example of the French poet José-Maria de Hérédia, whose influence is apparent, Rakić published only those of his poems in which he believed the emotion and the workmanship were adequate. During three decades of writing poetry, Rakić published only sixty poems. His poetry and his versification created a school in Serbian modern poetry. Thematically, his poems can be divided into lyrical love poems (*Love Poem, Sincere Poem, Serenade*), philosophical poems (*In Irons, The Abandoned Church*), and poems from the national past (*Simonida, Jefimija*).
PUBLICATIONS: *Pesme* (Beograd: 1904); *Nove Pesme* (Beograd: 1912); *Pesme M.M. Rakića* (Zagreb: 1924); *Pesme* (Beograd: 1936).

ŠANTIĆ, ALEKSA (1868-1924). As a poet and prominent cultural personality, Aleksa Šantić belongs to the poetic and cultural center of Mostar, Herzegovina. With the exception of two years (1881-1883) which Šantić spent on studies in Trieste and Ljubljana, Mostar remained the center of his life. As a young man, in the company of Jovan Dučić and Svetozar Ćorović, Šantić founded the patriotic choir *Gusle* and the literary review *Zora*. In the poems of his youth, Šantić was under the influence of the nineteenth-century Romantics, and later under that of Vojislav Ilić. His poetry is patriotic and lyrical but remains always deeply linked to his home town of Mostar. During World War I, the Austrians arrested Šantić and kept him hostage in Sarajevo. After the war, he returned to Mostar where he died in a difficult financial situation. Šantić was never attracted by life in foreign countries. Jovan Dučić, his close friend, persuaded him to move to Geneva, but Šantić returned home after a three-week stay. Besides his poems, Šantić published historical dramas and translations of foreign poets, mostly Heinrich Heine and Friedrich Schiller. **PUBLICATIONS:** *Pjesme* (Mostar: 1891); *Pjesme Alekse R. Šantića* (Mostar: 1895); *Pjesme* (Mostar: 1901); *Pod maglom, slika iz Gornje Hercegovine* (Beograd: 1907); *Pjesme* (Mostar: 1908); *Pjesme* (Beograd: 1911); *Hasanaginica, dramska slika u stihovima s pjevanjem* (Novi Sad: 1911); *Na starim ognjištima* (Mostar: 1913); *Pjesme* (Zagreb: 1918); *Pjesme* (Beograd: 1924). Translations: *Lirski intermeco, pjesme Hajnriha Hajnea* (Mostar: 1897); *Iz njemačke lirike* (Mostar: 1910); *Svatopluh Čeh: Pesme roba* (Sarajevo: 1919); *Fridrih Šiler: Viljem Tel* (Beograd: 1922).

STEFANOVIĆ, SVETISLAV (1874-1944). Stefanović finished the Medical School of the University in Vienna and served as a physician in provincial towns in Serbia. He returned to the University of Vienna where he studied Comparative Literature. Stefanović lived and worked in Belgrade. His poems bring new overtones of symbolism into Serbian poetry. Stefanović's poetry is very close to Impressionistic painting, as it deals with inner landscapes. A great part of Stefanović's work were translations, among which the most important are translations of Shakespeare's works (*Macbeth, Othello, King Lear, Julius Caesar, Hamlet*). He also published a series of literary essays, mostly on English authors. **PUBLICATIONS:** *Pesme* (Mostar: 1903); *Pesme* (Mostar: 1904); *Pesme* (Mostar: 1905); *Sunce i senke* (Beograd: 1912); *Strofe i ritmovi* (Beograd: 1919); *Granice* (Beograd: 1928). In prose Stefanović published: *Skice* (Beograd: 1904); *Pogledi i pokušaji* (Beograd: 1919); and dramas: *Sukobi* (Beograd: 1911) and *Kuća tamnih senki* (Beograd: 1927).

Index of Titles and First Lines in Serbo-Croatian

Index of Titles and First Lines in English Translation